The Best of SuperStitch

KNITTING PATTERNS

The Best of SuperStitch
KNITTING PATTERNS

Edited by Pam Dawson

ORBIS · LONDON

Acknowledgments

The photographs on the following pages are by courtesy of: Camera Press 11, 14, 16, 28, 48, 53, 61, 71, 89, 90, 112; French Wools (Pingouin) Limited 35, 97; Neveda Hand Knitting Yarns 25.
The remaining photographs were taken by the following photographers: Tom Belshaw, Chris Harvey, Liz McAulay, Tino Tedaldi and Nick Wright.
The pattern pieces were drawn by Colin Salmon.

Front cover: Liz McAulay
Half title page: Tom Belshaw
Title page: Camera Press
Back cover: Liz McAulay

First published in Great Britain by Orbis Publishing Limited, London 1986

This material previously appeared in the partwork *SuperStitch*

Printed in Italy

ISBN: 0-85613-984-X

Contents

Abbreviations   6
Introduction   7
Striped batwing cardigan   9
Cool cotton jersey   11
Cardigan and sun top   15
Rag knit top in butterfly pattern   17
Random-patterned jerseys   20
Batwing jersey in cool cotton   24
Jersey in garter stitch and rib checks   26
Lacy slipover   28
Double-breasted waistcoat   30
Cardigan or jersey with wavy stripes   33
Sparkling party top for evening   35
Mohair cardigan with pierrot collar   36
Soft, pretty jersey with flower motif   39
Entrelac jersey in mohair   43
Cardigan with woven clusters   45
Cable jacket   49
Stitch sampler jersey   53
Two-colour mohair jersey   54
Embroidered striped jersey   57
Striped jersey   59
Cable pattern coat   60
Fair Isle cardigan   63
Look-alike slipovers in authentic Fair Isle   65
Icelandic jerseys   69
Jacquard yoked jersey   71
Guernseys for a man or woman   75
Traditional woollen guernseys   79
Traditional Aran jersey   81
Aran sweaters   85
Norwegian-type cardigan   87
Norwegian-style jersey   91
Cricket pullover with cable panels   95
A new look for the traditional Argyle   96
Man's geometric patterned jersey   98
Raglan-sleeve jersey with pouch pocket   101
Zipped blouson-style jacket   103
Man's three-colour jersey   107
Fisherman's rib jerseys for the family   109
Man's striped jersey   113
Designer jersey for a man or woman   114
Choosing the right yarn   117
Standard aftercare symbols   119
Index   120

Knitting pattern abbreviations

alt	alternate(ly)	patt	pattern
approx	approximate(ly)	psso	pass slipped stitch over
beg	begin(ning)	p2sso	pass 2 slipped stitches over
ch	chain(s)	P	purl
cm	centimetre(s)	P up	pick up and purl
cont	continu(e)(ing)	P-wise	purlwise direction
cr2L	cross 1 knit st to left	rem	remain(ing)
cr2R	cross 1 knit st to right	rep	repeat(ing)
dec	decreas(e)(ing)	Rs	right side of fabric
foll	follow(ing)	sl	slip
g st	garter stitch	sl st	slip stitch(es)
g	gramme(s)	st(s)	stitch(es)
inc	increas(e)(ing) by working twice into a stitch	st st	stocking stitch
K	knit	tog	together
		tw2B	twist 2 knit stitches to left
K up	pick up and knit, as round neck edge	tw2F	twist 2 knit stitches to right
		tw2PB	twist 2 purl stitches to left
K-wise	knitwise direction	tw2PF	twist 2 purl stitches to right
m	metre(s)	Ws	wrong side of fabric
MB	make bobble, as specified	ybk	yarn back between needles
mm	millimetre(s)	yfwd	yarn forward between needles
M1	make one by picking up loop lying between needles and knit through back of loop to increase one	yon	yarn over needle
		yrn	yarn around needle

Pattern symbols

An asterisk, *, in a pattern row denotes that the stitches after this sign must be repeated from that point to the end of the row, or to the last number of stitches given.

Instructions shown in round brackets, (), denote that this section of the pattern is to be worked for all sizes. Instructions shown in square brackets, [], denote larger sizes.

Introduction

Knitted garments are now acknowledged to play such an important role in the fashion scene that it is difficult to believe they were ever considered 'granny gear'. To the discerning fashion eye, however, hand-knitting has never gone out of style, and each generation has produced its own interpretation of the basic classics. Jersey designs are fundamentally ageless and all that varies to any degree is the type of yarn available in the shops, the fashion colours and textures of the moment, the emphasis on certain focal points, such as sleeves or necklines, and the current popularity of particular stitch patterns.

This book includes something for everyone: simple knits for the beginner and complex techniques for the enthusiast; traditional classics for the devotee and high-fashion looks for all occasions; economy-inspired or unashamedly luxurious designs; plus a selection of unisex garments for you and the man in your life.

All the information you need to make a success of your knitting is here. There are details of the exact fibre content of the yarns used; pattern-piece diagrams giving the overall measurements of a garment, including tolerance; alternative colour-ways and a number of useful 'professional touches'. Pay particular attention to the section on choosing the right yarn (see page 117). If you have to purchase a substitute, make sure it has approximately the same fibre content and that it will work to the same tension, otherwise you will not obtain satisfactory results.

Now that the ready-to-wear trade has discovered knitting, what was once considered a cottage industry has become big business. Everywhere you look, you see commercially machine-knitted garments, but even the simplest can cost up to twice as much as if you knitted it for yourself. And if you look in the shops for the real thing – a genuine hand-knit – you are thinking in terms of hundreds of pounds.

Why not rediscover the pleasure you can derive from this simple skill, the money you will save in the process, and the pride that comes from creating a genuine hand-knit of your own?

Pam Dawson, 1986

Striped batwing cardigan

Bold stripes run vertically on this low-buttoning, batwing cardigan. The main section is worked in stocking stitch in one piece, from cuff to cuff. The ribbed welts and neckband are knitted afterwards.

Sizes

To fit 81 [86:91:97]cm/32 [34:36:38]in bust
Length to centre back neck, 52 [53:54:55]cm/20½ [20¾:21¼:21¾]in
Sleeve seam, 52 [52:53:53]cm/20½ [20½:20¾:20¾]in
The figures in [] refer to the 86/34, 91/36 and 97cm/38in sizes respectively

You will need

4 [4:4:5]×50g balls of Neveda Brenda (78% cotton, 22% viscose) in main colour A
3 [3:3:4] balls of same in contrast colour B

Left: A sequence of wide and narrow stripes creates a striking effect on this sideways-knitted cardigan.
Below: A wide band is worked in the main colour down the centre back, before working the stripes in reverse order.

2 [3:3:3] balls each of same in contrast colours C and D
One pair 3mm/No 11 needles
One pair 4mm/No 8 needles
Set of four 3mm/No 11 needles pointed at both ends
Three buttons

Tension

18 sts and 24 rows to 10cm/4in over st st worked on 4mm/No 8 needles

Cardigan body and sleeves

With 3mm/No 11 needles and A cast on 40 [42:42:44] sts and beg at left cuff, noting that the body and sleeves are worked in one piece.
Work 5cm/2in K1, P1 rib.
Change to 4mm/No 8 needles.
Next row (inc row) K 3 [4:4:5] sts, inc in next st, (K10, inc in next st) 3 times, K3 [4:4:5] sts. 44 [46:46: 48] sts.
Beg with a P row cont in st st, inc one st at each end of every foll 4th row until there are 92 [96:96:100] sts, marking each end of last inc row with coloured markers, *at the same time* when 2 [4:8:10] rows in A have been completed, beg striped patt, as foll:

4 rows C, 2 rows A, 4 rows C, 2 rows B, 4 rows C, 12 rows B, 4 rows D, 2 rows B, 4 rows D, 2 rows A, 4 rows D, 12 rows A.
These 56 rows form striped patt. Cont in striped patt without shaping until work measures 52 [52:53:53]cm/20½ [20½:20¾:20¾]in from beg, ending with a Ws row.

Back and left front
At beg of next and foll row cast on 38 [38:40:40] sts. 168 [172:176:180] sts.
Keeping striped patt correct work 13 [14:14.5:15.5]cm/5 [5½:5¾:6]in measured from top of sleeve, ending with a Ws row.

Back
Next row K82 [84:86:88] sts, turn and leave rem sts on spare needle.
Next row (dec row) Cast off one st, P to end.
Cont to end of 3rd striped patt rep, then work extra rows in A only, until neck edge measures 9 [9:9.5:9.5]cm/3½ [3½:3¾:3¾]in, ending with a Ws row.
Mark each end of last row to denote centre back.
Work same number of rows with A to marked row, then cont in striped patt, reversing patt as foll:
4 rows D, 2 rows A, 4 rows D, 2 rows B, 4 rows D, 12 rows B, 4 rows C, 2 rows B, 4 rows C, 2 rows A, 4 rows C, 12 rows A.
Cont until work measures same as from marked centre point to dec st

at neck edge, ending at neck edge.
Next row (inc row) Cast on one st, patt to end.
Leave these sts on spare needle. Break off yarn.

Left front
With Rs of work facing rejoin yarn to rem 86 [88:90:92] sts for left front. Keeping stripe patt correct throughout, shape neck by casting off at beg of next and every alt row 6 sts 7 times, 6 [6:5:5] sts 3 times, 0 [0:5:5] sts once and 26 [28:28:30] sts once.

Right front
With 4mm/No 8 needles and A cast on 26 [28:28:30] sts. P one row.
Work as given for left front, reversing striped patt and shaping by casting on at neck edge on every alt row 0 [0:5:5] sts once, 6 [6:5:5] sts 3 times and 6 sts 7 times, ending with a Rs row. 86 [88:90:92] sts.

Right front and back
Keeping patt correct as now set work across sts of right front then across sts of back. 168 [172:176:180] sts.
Cont until work measures 13 [14:14.5:15.5]cm/5 [5½:5¾:6]in from join of right front and back, ending with a Ws row.
At beg of next and foll row cast off 38 [38:40:40] sts. 92 [96:96:100] sts.
Cont in striped patt until work measures same from cast off sts to markers at each end of last inc row

on left sleeve, ending with a Ws row.
Dec one st at each end of next and every foll 4th row until there are 44 [46:46:48] sts.
Work 2 rows without shaping.
Next row (dec row) P3 [4:4:5] sts, P2 tog, (P10, P2 tog) 3 times, P3 [4:4:5] sts. 40 [42:42:44] sts.
Change to 3mm/No 11 needles.
Work 5cm/2in K1, P1 rib. Cast off in rib.

Waistband
Join side and sleeve seams. With Rs of work facing, 3mm/No 11 needles and A, pick up and K an even number of sts along lower edge of body, picking up 3 sts from every 4 row ends.
Work 5cm/2in K1, P1 rib. Cast off in rib.

Front edges and neckband
With Rs of work facing, set of four 3mm/No 11 needles and A, pick up and K an odd number of sts along right front edge, round neck and along left front edge, picking up 5 sts from every 6 row ends of ribbing, 10 sts from every 9 cast on or off sts up straight edges of front, one st from every st or row end of neck shaping, then 5 sts to every 6 row ends round back neck.
Next row (Ws) P1, *K1, P1, rep from * to end.
Work 2 more rows rib as now set.
Next row (buttonhole row) Rib 3 sts, cast off 3 sts, (rib 10 [11:11:12] sts, cast off 3 sts) twice, rib to end.
Next row Rib to end, casting on 3 sts above those cast off in previous row.
Work 3 more rows in rib.
Next row (foldline) K to end.
Work 3 more rows rib.
Next row (buttonhole row) Rib to last 32 [34:34:36] sts, (cast off 3 sts, rib 10 [11:11:12] sts) twice, cast off 3 sts, rib 3 sts.
Next row Rib to end casting on 3 sts above those cast off in previous row.
Work 3 rows rib. Cast off loosely in rib.

To make up
Press under a dry cloth with a cool iron.
Fold front and neckband in half to Ws and sl st down. Sew round double buttonholes. Sew on buttons.

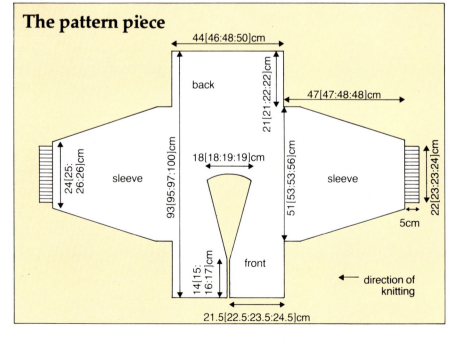

The pattern piece

44[46:48:50]cm

back

47[47:48:48]cm

21[21:22:22]cm

sleeve

93[95:97:100]cm

18[18:19:19]cm

51[53:53:56]cm

sleeve

24[25:26:26]cm

22[23:23:24]cm

14[15:16:17]cm

front

5cm

← direction of knitting

21.5[22.5:23.5:24.5]cm

Cool cotton jersey

This jersey with its pretty, full sleeves is worthy of a place in any leisure-wear wardrobe.

The clusters of grapes 'growing' up and over the right shoulder and down the right sleeve are knitted in to the fabric of the garment. The leaves are embroidered on afterwards . . . here they have been worked in three contrasting colours of embroidery silk but could be worked in one only, if you prefer.

Crocheted picot edging at the neckline adds a crisp finishing flourish.

Below: Knitted in cool cotton this jersey is a fairly simple shape. The picot edge can be omitted if you prefer.

Sizes

To fit 86 [91:97] cm bust
Length to shoulder, 60 [61:62] cm
Sleeve seam, 30 cm
The figures in [] refer to the 91 and 97cm sizes respectively

You will need

8 [9:9] × 50g balls of DMC Pearl Coton No. 4 (100% cotton), in main colour A
2 skeins each of embroidery silk or cotton in each of 3 contrast colours, B, C and D for leaves
One pair 3mm needles
One pair 3¾mm needles
One 3.00mm crochet hook

Tension

24 sts and 32 rows to 10cm over st st worked on 3¾mm needles

Back

With 3mm needles and A cast on 102 [106:114] sts.
1st row (Rs) K2, *P2, K2, rep from * to end.
2nd row P2, *K2, P2, rep from * to end.
Rep these 2 rows for 6cm, ending with a Rs row.
Next row (inc row) Rib 6 [5:7] sts, *M1, rib 9 [8:10] sts, rep from * 9 [11:9] times more, M1, rib 6 [5:7] sts. 113 [119:125] sts. **

Change to 3¾mm needles. Beg with a K row cont in st st until work measures 40cm from beg, ending with a P row.

Shape armholes

Cast off at beg of next and every row 4 sts twice, 3 sts twice and 2 sts 4 times. Dec one st at each end of next and every alt row until 85 [89:93] sts rem. Cont without shaping until armholes measure 20 [21:22] cm from beg, ending with a P row.

Shape shoulders

Cast off at beg of next and every row 8 sts 4 times and 8 [9:10] sts twice.
Leave rem 37 [39:41] sts on holder for centre back neck.

Front

Work as given for back to **.
Change to 3¾mm needles.
Commence bunch of grapes bobble patt.
1st row (Rs) K30 [33:36] sts, make bobble by K into front, back, front, back and front of next st, making 5 sts, (turn, P5, turn, K5) twice, lift 2nd, 3rd, 4th and 5th sts over first st and off needle – **called MB**, K to end.
Beg with a P row work 3 rows st st.

5th row K28 [31:34] sts, MB, K3, MB, K to end.
Beg with a P row work 3 rows st st.
9th row K30 [33:36] sts, MB, K3, MB, K to end.
Beg with a P row work 3 rows st st.
13th row K28 [31:34] sts, MB, (K3, MB) twice, K to end.
Beg with a P row work 3 rows st st.
17th row K26 [29:32] sts, MB, (K3, MB) 3 times, K to end.
Beg with a P row work 3 rows st st.
21st row K24 [27:30] sts, MB, (K3, MB) 4 times, K to end.
Beg with a P row work 3 rows st st.
25th row K22 [25:28] sts, MB, (K3, MB) 5 times, K to end.
Beg with a P row work 3 rows st st.
29th row K20 [23:26] sts, MB, (K3, MB) 6 times, K to end.
Beg with a P row work 3 rows st st.
33rd row K26 [29:32] sts, MB, (K3, MB) 4 times, K to end.
Beg with a P row work 3 rows st st.
37th row K28 [31:34] sts, MB, (K3, MB) 4 times, K to end.
Beg with a P row work 3 rows st st.
41st row As 33rd.
Beg with a P row work 3 rows st st.
45th row K28 [31:34] sts, MB, (K3, MB) twice, K15, beg 2nd bunch of grapes with MB, K to end.
Beg with a P row work 3 rows st st.
49th row K30 [33:36] sts, MB, K3, MB, K15, for 2nd bunch of grapes MB, K3, MB, K to end.
Beg with a P row work 3 rows st st.
53rd row K52 [55:58] sts noting that first bunch of grapes has been completed, MB, K3, MB for 2nd bunch of grapes, K to end.
Beg with a P row work 3 rows st st.
Cont working 2nd bunch of grapes to match first bunch, beg bobble patt with 13th row and working 3 rows st st between each bobble patt row until 41st bobble patt row has been completed. Cont working 3 rows st st between each bobble patt row.
89th row K50 [53:56] sts, MB, (K3, MB) twice, K15, beg 3rd bunch of grapes with MB, K to end.
93rd row K52 [55:58] sts, MB, K3, MB, K15, for 3rd bunch of grapes MB, K3, MB, K to end.
2nd bunch of grapes has now been completed. Cont working 3rd bunch of grapes to match first bunch, beg bobble patt with 9th row, *at the same time* shape armholes when work measures 40cm from beg, ending with a Ws row.

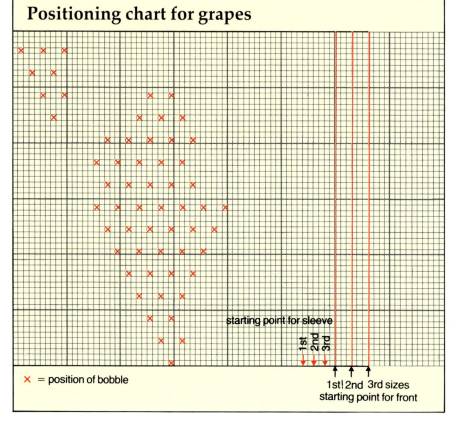

Positioning chart for grapes

× = position of bobble

starting point for sleeve

1st 2nd 3rd

1st 2nd 3rd sizes
starting point for front

Shape armholes

Keeping patt correct throughout, cast off at beg of next and every row 4 sts twice, 3 sts twice and 2 sts 4 times. Dec one st at each end of next and every alt row until 85 [89:93] sts rem. When 3rd bunch of grapes has been completed, cont without shaping until armholes measure 12 [13:14] cm from beg, ending with a Ws row.

Shape neck

Next row K34 [35:36] sts, turn and leave rem sts on holder.
Complete left shoulder first. Cast off at beg of next and every alt row 3 sts once, 2 sts twice and one st 3 times. 24 [25:26] sts.
Cont without shaping until armhole measures same as back to shoulder, ending with a Ws row.

Shape shoulder

Cast off at beg of next and every alt row 8 sts twice and 8 [9:10] sts once.
With Rs of work facing, leave first 17 [19:21] sts on holder for centre front neck, rejoin yarn to rem sts and K to end. P one row.
Complete to match first side, reversing all shapings.

Right sleeve

With 3mm needles and A cast on 66 [66:70] sts. Work 6cm rib as given for back, ending with a Rs row.
Next row (inc row) Rib 1 [8:10] sts, *M1, rib 3 [2:2] sts, rep from * 20 [24:24] times, M1, rib 2 [8:10] sts. 88 [92:96] sts.
Change to 3¾mm needles. Beg with

Right: Close up view of the grape motif showing the positioning and shape of the leaves for embroidery.

a K row work 2 rows st st.**
Commence bunch of grapes bobble patt.
1st row K24 [26:28] sts, MB, K to end.
Beg with a P row work 3 rows st st.
5th row K22 [24:26] sts, MB, K3, MB, K to end.
Beg with a P row work 3 rows st st. Cont to work first bunch of grapes as given for front, beg bobble patt with 9th row and working 3 rows st st between each bobble patt row until 44th row has been completed.
45th row K22 [24:26] sts, MB, (K3, MB) twice, K15, beg 2nd bunch of grapes with MB, K to end.
Beg with a P row work 3 rows st st.
49th row K24 [26:28] sts, MB, K3, MB, K15, for 2nd bunch of grapes MB, K3, MB, K to end.
Beg with a P row work 3 rows st st.
53rd row K46 [48:50] sts noting that first bunch of grapes has been completed, MB, K3, MB for 2nd bunch of grapes, K to end.
Beg with a P row work 3 rows st st. Cont working 2nd bunch of grapes to match first bunch, beg bobble patt with 13th row and working 3 rows st st between each bobble patt row, *at the same time* shape top when sleeve measures 30cm from beg, ending with a Ws row.

Shape top

Cast off at beg of next and every row 2 sts 14 times, one st 18 [20:22]

times, 2 sts 6 times, 3 sts 4 times, 4 sts twice and 10 [12:14] sts once.

Left sleeve

Work as given for right sleeve to **
Cont in st st only and complete as given for right sleeve.

Neckband

Join right shoulder seam. With Rs of work facing, 3mm needles and A pick up and K18 sts down left front neck, K across front neck sts on holder, pick up and K18 sts up right front neck then K across back neck sts on holder. 90 [94:98] sts.
Beg with a 2nd row work 2.5cm rib as given for back. Cast off loosely in rib.

To make up

Press each piece lightly under a damp cloth with a warm iron, taking care not to flatten bobble patt.
Embroider leaves at top of each bunch of grapes in three colours and chain st, as illustrated.
Join left shoulder and neckband seam. Sew in sleeves.
Neck edging With Rs of work facing and 3.00mm hook work one round of dc all round neck edge. Join with a ss to first dc.
Next round 2ch to count as first dc, miss first dc, 1dc into next dc, *3ch, 1dc into first of these 3ch, 1dc into next dc, rep from * to end. Join with a ss to 2nd of first 2ch. Fasten off. Press seams.

The pattern pieces

sleeve
36[38:40]cm
14[15:16]cm
24cm
6cm
27.5[27.5:29]cm

15[16:17]cm 10[10.5:11]cm
35[37:39]cm
12[13:14]cm
20[21:22]cm
front/back
34cm
6cm
47[49.5:52]cm
42.5[44:47.5]cm

Cardigan and summer top

The cardigan has square set-in sleeves which eliminate the need for complicated shaping, and the suntop has a picot edging.

Sizes

To fit 81 [86:91:97]cm bust
Cardigan length to shoulder, 57 [58:59:60]cm
Sleeve seam, 43 [44:45:46]cm
Top length to underarm, 33.5cm
The figures in [] refer to the 86, 91 and 97cm sizes respectively

You will need

Cardigan 4 [4:5:5]×50g balls of Phildar Luxe (85% acrylic, 15% wool), in main colour A
1 [1:2:2] balls of same in each of contrasts B, C, D and E
Top 2 [2:2:2] balls of same in main colour A
1 [1:1:1] ball of same in contrast B
One pair 2¾mm needles
One pair 3mm needles

Tension

30 sts and 40 rows to 10cm over st st worked on 3mm needles

Cardigan back

With 2¾mm needles and A, cast on 129 [137:145:153] sts.
1st row P1, *K1, P1, rep from * to end.
2nd row K1, *P1, K1, rep from * to end.
Rep these 2 rows for 3cm, ending with a 2nd row.
Change to 3mm needles. Beg with a P row cont in reversed st st working in stripes of 2 rows B, 2 rows A, 2 rows C, 2 rows A, 2 rows D, 2 rows A, 2 rows E and 2 rows A. **
These 16 rows form the striped sequence throughout but, *at the same time* work bobbles on next and every foll 20th row as foll:
17th row P4, *insert right-hand needle knitwise into next st but on 4th row below, (K1, yfwd, K1, yfwd, K1, yfwd, K1) all into this st, sl the 7 loops back on to left-hand needle and K them tog with the next st tbl – **called MB**, P7, rep from * to last 5 sts, MB. P4.
Cont in striped patt working bobbles on every foll 20th row until work measures 38cm/15in from beg, ending with a Ws row.

Shape armholes

Keeping patt correct throughout, cast off 16 [16:18:18] sts at beg of next 2 rows. 97 [105:109:117] sts.
Cont without shaping until armholes measure 19 [20:21:22]cm from beg, ending with a Ws row.

Shape shoulders

Cast off at beg of next and every row 7 [7:8:8] sts 6 times, 6 [9:7:10] sts twice and 43 [45:47:49] sts once.

Cardigan left front

With 2¾mm needles and A, cast on 63 [67:71:75] sts and work as given for back to **.
17th row P4, *MB, P7, rep from * to last 3 [7:3:7] sts, MB, P2 [6:2:6].
Cont in patt as now set until work measures same as back to underarm, ending with a Ws row.

Shape armhole

Cast off 16 [16:18:18] sts at beg of next row. 47 [51:53:57] sts.
Cont without shaping until armhole measures 14 [15:15:16]cm from beg, ending with a Ws row.

Shape neck

Cast off at beg of next and every alt row 7 [7:8:8] sts once, 3 sts twice, 2 sts twice and one st 3 [4:4:5] times. 27 [30:31:34] sts.
Cont without shaping until armhole measures same as back to shoulder, ending with a Ws row.

Shape shoulder

Cast off at beg of next and every alt row 7 [7:8:8] sts 3 times and 6 [9:7:10] sts once.

Cardigan right front

Work as given for left front, reversing all shaping and bobble patt row, as foll:
17th row P2 [6:2:6] sts, *MB, P7, rep from * to last 5 sts, MB, P4.

Cardigan sleeves

With 2¾mm needles and A, cast on 59 [61:65:67] sts. Work in rib as given for back for 8cm, ending with a 1st row.
Next row (inc row) Rib 2 [0:4:2] sts, *K twice into next st, P1, rep from * to last st, K1. 87 [91:95:99] sts.
Change to 3mm needles. Work 16 rows striped patt as given for back, inc one st at each end of 7th and 15th rows. 91 [95:99:103] sts.
17th row P1 [3:5:7] sts, *MB, P7, rep from * to last 2 [4:6:8] sts, MB, P to end.
Cont in patt as now set, inc one st at

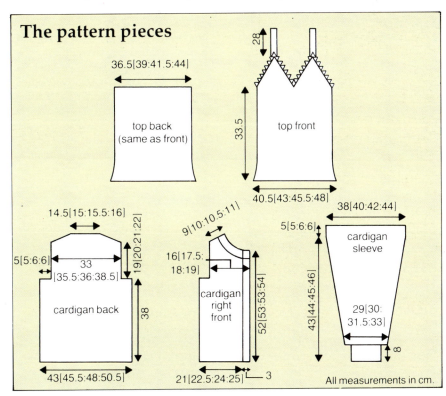

The pattern pieces

36.5[39:41.5:44]

top back (same as front)

28

top front

33.5

40.5[43:45.5:48]

14.5[15:15.5:16]

19[20:21:22]

5[5:6:6]

33 [35.5:36:38.5]

cardigan back

38

43[45.5:48:50.5]

9[10:10.5:11]

16[17.5: 18:19]

cardigan right front

52[53:53:54]

21[22.5:24:25]

3

5[5:6:6]

38[40:42:44]

cardigan sleeve

43[44:45:46]

29[30: 31.5:33]

8

All measurements in cm.

each end of every 8th row until there are 115 [121:127:133] sts. Cont without shaping until sleeve measures 43 [44:45:46]cm from beg. Place a marker at each end of last row, then cont in patt for a further 5 [5:6:6]cm ending with a Ws row. Cast off loosely.

Cardigan neckband

Join shoulder seams. With 2¾mm needles, A and Rs of work facing, pick up and K111 [115:119:123] sts evenly round neck. Beg with a 2nd row work 10cm rib as given for back. Cast off in rib.

Cardigan front bands

With 2¾mm needles, A and Rs of work facing, pick up and K171 [175:175:179] sts evenly along right front edge from cast-on edge to halfway up side of neckband. Beg with a 2nd row work 3cm rib as given for back. Cast off in rib. Work along left front edge in same way, beg halfway down side of neckband to cast-on edge.

Top back

With 2¾mm needles and B, cast on 121 [129:137:145] sts.
**Beg with a K row work 6 rows st st.
7th row (eyelet hole row) K1, *yfwd, K2 tog, rep from * to end. Beg with a P row work 6 rows st st. ** Break off B. Change to 3mm needles. Join in A and P one row. Beg with a P row cont in reversed st st, dec one st at each end of 7th and every foll 8th row until 109 [117:125:133] sts rem. Cont without shaping until work measures 32cm from eyelet hole row, ending with a K row. *** Break off A. Change to 2¾mm needles. Join in B and rep from ** to **. Cast off.

Top front

Work as given for back to ***.

Shape front neck

Next row P54 [58:62:66] sts, turn and leave rem sts on holder. Complete left side first. Dec one st at each end of every row until 2 sts rem. Break off yarn. Leave 2 sts on a

safety pin.
With Rs of work facing sl first st on to a safety pin and leave for centre neck, rejoin A to rem sts and P to end.
Complete to match left side.

Front edging

With 2¾mm needles, B and Rs facing, * pick up and K26 [28:30:32] sts up side of point, K2 tog the sts on safety pin, pick up and K26 [28:30:32] sts down other side of point, *, K centre st from safety pin, then rep from * to * along other point.
Next row P26 [28:30:32] sts, inc one by picking up loop between sts and P tbl – **called inc 1P**, P1, inc 1P, P to next point, inc 1P, P1, inc 1P, P to end.
Next row K27 [29:31:33] sts, inc one by picking up loop between sts and K tbl – **called inc 1K**, K1, inc 1K, K to one st before centre st, sl 1, K2 tog, psso, K to next point, inc 1K, K1, inc 1K, K to end.
Keeping the number of sts correct between shapings, rep last 2 rows once more, then first of them again.
Next row (eyelet hole row) K1, *yfwd, K2 tog, rep from * to end.
Next row P to one st before point, P3 tog, P to one st before next point, P3 tog, P to end.
Next row K to one st before point, K3 tog, K to centre, inc 1K, K1, inc 1K, K to next point, K3 tog, K to end.
Keeping the number of sts correct between shapings, rep last 2 rows twice more. Cast off.

Straps (make 2)

With 2¾mm needles and B, cast on 9 sts. Work in rib as given for cardigan back for 28cm, or length required. Cast off.

To make up

Press all pieces lightly under a dry cloth with a cool iron.
Cardigan Set in sleeves, sewing last part of sleeves from markers to cast off sts of armholes. Join side and sleeve seams. Fold neckband in half to Ws and sl st down. Press seams.
Top Join side and edging seams. Fold edges in half to Ws and sl st down. Sew on straps. Press seams.

Rag knit top in butterfly pattern

An unusual rag-like cotton yarn turns this simple top into something special. Using extra-large needles makes it quick to knit, with a simple slip stitch pattern forming the butterfly motifs. Garter stitch is used for the narrow welt, sleeve and neck edges.

Sizes

To fit 86 [91:97]cm/34 [36:38]in bust
Length to shoulder, 48cm/19in
Sleeve seam, 33cm/13in
The figures in [] refer to the 91/36 and 97cm/38in sizes respectively

You will need

10 [11:11]×50g balls of Pingouin Biais de Coton (100% cotton)
One pair 9mm/No 00 needles
One pair 10mm/No 000 needles

Tension

10 sts and 14 rows to 10cm/4in over patt worked on 10mm/No 000 needles

Note

The yarn has a tendency to twist as it is being knitted; untwist it at the end of every row or you will affect the tension and the quantity used

Back

With 9mm/No 00 needles cast on 52 [54:56] sts.
K 3 rows g st.
Change to 10mm/No 000 needles.
Commence butterfly patt.
1st row (Rs) K1 [2:3] sts, *yfwd, holding yarn loosely across front of work sl next 5 sts in a P-wise direction, ybk, K5, rep from * 4 times more, K1 [2:3] sts.
2nd row P to end.
3rd to 8th rows Rep 1st and 2nd rows 3 times more.
9th row K3 [4:5] sts, *insert the right-hand needle upwards under the 4 loops stranded across the front of the work, yarn round the needle and draw a loop through, keep this loop on the right-hand needle then K the next st from the left-hand needle, lift the 2nd st on the right-hand needle over the first and off the needle – **called LK1**, K9, rep from * 3 times more, LK1, K8 [9:10] sts.

10th row As 2nd.
11th row K6 [7:8] sts, *yfwd, holding yarn loosely across front of work sl next 5 sts in a P-wise direction, ybk, K5, rep from * 3 times more, yfwd, holding yarn loosely across front of work sl next 5 sts in a P-wise direction, ybk, K1 [2:3] sts.
12th row As 2nd.
13th to 18th rows Rep 11th and 12th rows 3 times more.
19th row K8 [9:10] sts, *LK1, K9, rep from * 3 times more, LK1, K3 [4:5] sts.
20th row As 2nd.
These 20 rows form the patt.
Rep patt rows 3 times more when work should measure about 44.5cm/17½in from beg.
K 4 rows g st. Cast off loosely.

Front

Work as given for back.

Sleeves

With 9mm/No 00 needles cast on 34 [36:38] sts.
K 3 rows g st.
Change to 10mm/No 000 needles.
Commence patt.
1st row (Rs) K2 [3:4] sts, *yfwd, holding yarn loosely across front of work sl next 5 sts in a P-wise direction, ybk, K5, rep from * twice more, K2 [3:4] sts.

2nd row P to end.
3rd to 8th rows Rep 1st and 2nd rows 3 times more.
9th row K4 [5:6] sts, *LK1, K9, rep from * once more, LK1, K9 [10:11] sts.
10th row As 2nd.
11th row K7 [8:9] sts, *yfwd, holding yarn loosely across front of work sl next 5 sts in a P-wise direction, ybk, K5, rep from * once more, yfwd, holding yarn loosely across front of work sl next 5 sts in a P-wise direction, ybk, K2 [3:4] sts.
12th row As 2nd.
13th to 18th rows Rep 11th and 12th rows 3 times more.
19th row K9 [10:11] sts, *LK1, K9, rep from * once more, LK1, K4 [5:6]

Above: Stitch sample shows close-up detail of the butterfly pattern.

sts.
20th row As 2nd.
These 20 rows form patt.
Rep patt rows twice more when work should measure about 33cm/13in from beg. Cast off loosely.

To make up

Do not press as this will flatten patt. Join shoulder seams, using a double strand of matching sewing cotton and leaving an opening of about 25cm/9¾in in centre for neck.
Sew in sleeves with centre of top to shoulder seam. Join side and sleeve seams.

The pattern pieces

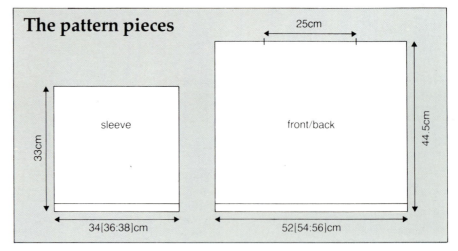

sleeve

33cm

34[36:38]cm

front/back

25cm

44.5cm

52[54:56]cm

Below: Choose a vibrant colour or the cool, classic shade shown opposite, either looks great for this stylish top.

Random-patterned jerseys

To please young fashion followers there's a choice of nine sizes for these unusual jerseys.

They are knitted in a bouclé yarn, in reverse stocking stitch, with random areas of plain stocking stitch worked in a contrast.

Sizes

To fit 66 [71:76:81:86:91:97:102:107]cm/26 [28:30:32:34:36:38:40:42]in bust/chest loosely

Length to shoulder, 38 [46:50:54:58:58:59:59:60]cm/15 [18:19¾:21¼:22¾:22¾:23¼:23¼:23½]in

Sleeve seam, 30 [34:38:42:43:44:45:46:48]cm/11¾ [13½:15:16½:17:17¼:17¾:18:19]in

The figures in [] refer to the 71/28, 76/30, 81/32, 86/34, 91/36, 97/38. 102/40 and 107cm/42in sizes respectively

You will need

4 [5:7:8:8:8:9:9:10]×50g balls of Argyll Cotton On (64% cotton, 31% acrylic, 5% nylon] in main colour A

1 [1:1:1:2:2:2:2:2] balls of same in contrast colour B

One pair 3mm/No 11 needles
One pair 3¾mm/No 9 needles

Tension

22 sts and 30 rows to 10cm/4in over st st worked on 3¾mm/No 9 needles

Note

Use separate balls of yarn for each contrast area, always twisting yarns at back of work when changing colour to avoid a hole; where more than 5 extra sts are worked in a colour, break off yarn and rejoin as necessary

Back

With 3mm/No 11 needles and A cast on 74 [78:82:86:94:98:102:106:110] sts.

1st row (Rs) P2, *K2, P2, rep from * to end.

2nd row K2, *P2, K2, rep from * to end.

Rep these 2 rows until work measures 5cm/2in from beg, ending with a 1st row.

Next row (inc row) Rib 4 [6:2:4:10:12:6:4:6] sts, *pick up loop lying between needles and K tbl – **called M1**, rib 6 [6:6:6:4:4:4:4:4] sts, rep from * 10 [10:12:12:18:18:22:24:24] times more, M1, rib 4 [6:2:4:8:10:4:2:4[sts. 86 [90:96:100:114:118:126:132:136] sts.

Change to 3¾mm/No 9 needles.
Commence random striped patt.

1st row (Rs) With A, P to end.
2nd row With A, K to end.
3rd row With first ball of A, P3 [5:8:10:17:19:23:26:28] sts, with B, K10 sts, with 2nd ball of A, P73 [75:78:80:87:89:93:96:98] sts.
4th row With 2nd ball of A, K68 [70:73:75:82:84:88:91:93] sts, with B, P15 sts, with first ball of A, K3 [5:8:10:17:19:23:26:28] sts.

Beg with 5th row, cont in patt from chart until 98 [122:134:146:160:160:162:162:164] rows have been completed.

Shape shoulders

Next row Keeping patt correct, cast off 30 [31:33:33:38:40:43:46:47] sts, P26 [28:30:34:38:38:40:40:42] sts and leave these sts on holder for centre back neck, cast off rem 30 [31:33:33:38:40:43:46:47] sts.

Front

Work as given for back until 80 [104:116:126:140:140:140:140:140] rows have been completed.

Shape neck

Next row Keeping patt correct, patt 38 [39:41:42:47:49:53:56:58] sts, turn and leave rem sts on spare needle.

Complete left shoulder first. Work one row in patt.

Dec one st at neck edge on next and every foll alt row until 30 [31:33:33:38:40:43:46:47] sts rem, ending with a Ws row. Cast off.

With Rs of work facing, sl first 10 [12:14:16:20:20:20:20:20] sts on to holder and leave for centre front neck, rejoin yarn to rem sts and pat to end.

Complete right shoulder to match left, reversing all shapings.

Sleeves

With 3mm/No 11 needles and A cast on 34 [38:38:38:42:46:46:50:50] sts. Work 5cm/2in rib as given for back, ending with a 1st row.

Next row (inc row) Rib 1 [4:3:3:6:9:8:11:10] sts, (M1, rib 1) 12 [11:12:12:11:10:11:10:11] times, rib 8 sts, (rib 1, M1) 12 [11:12:12:11:10:11:10:11] times, rib 1 [4:3:3:6:9:8:11:10] sts. 58 [60:62:62:64:66:68:70:72] sts.

Change to 3¾mm/No 9 needles.

Beg with a P row, work in patt as given on chart, inc one st at each end of every 8th [8th:6th:6th:6th:6th:6th:6th:6th] rows until there are 72 [80:86:92:96:102:106:110:114] sts.

Cont in patt without shaping until 76 [88:100:112:114:118:120:124:130] rows have been completed. Cast off loosely.

Neckband

Join right shoulder seam.

With Rs of work facing, 3mm/No 11 needles and A, pick up and K15 [15:15:16:16:16:17:17:18] sts down left side of neck, K across front neck sts on holder, pick up and K15 [15:15:16:16:16:17:17:18] sts up right side of neck and K across back neck sts on holder. 66 [70:74:82:90:90:94:94:98] sts.

Beg with a 2nd row work 5cm/2in rib as given for back. Cast off very loosely in rib.

To make up

Do not press.
Join left shoulder and neckband seam. Fold neckband in half to Ws and sl st down.
Place centre of sleeve to shoulder seam and sew in sleeve. Join side and sleeve seams.

Chart for front and back

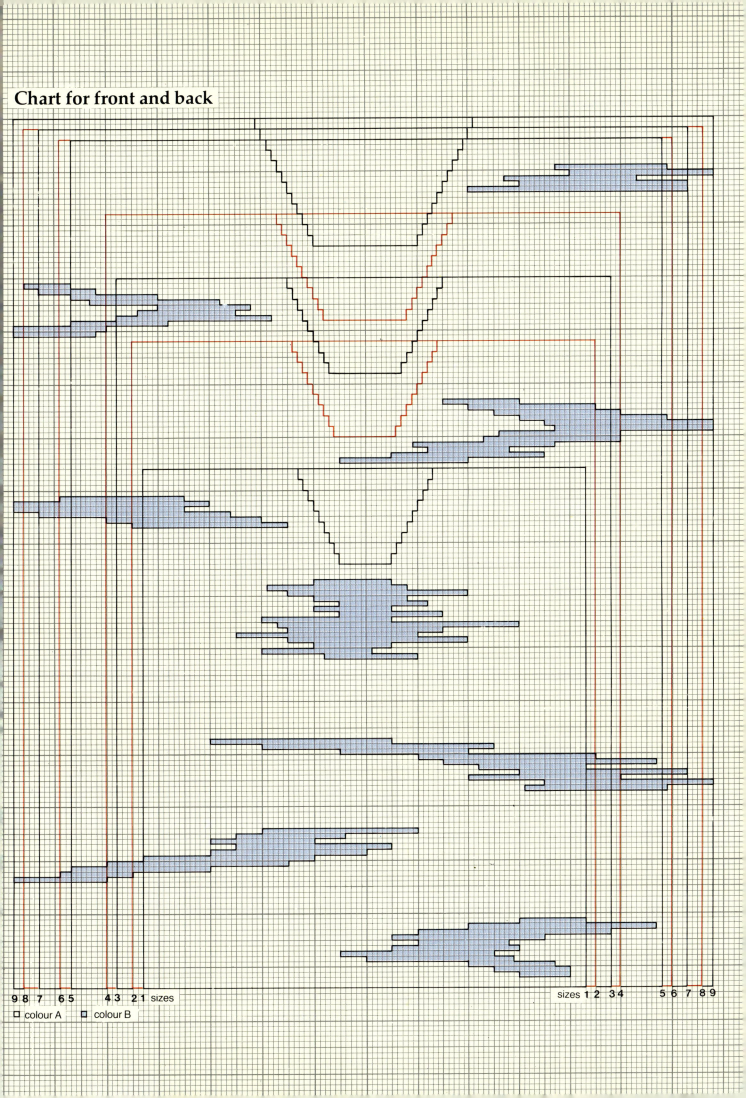

Chart for sleeve

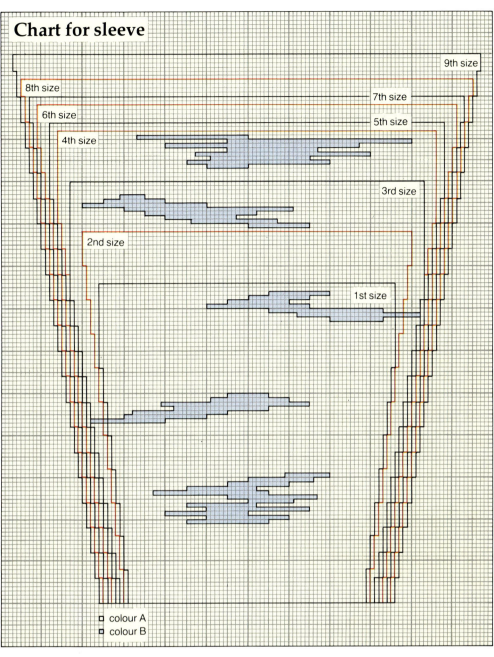

9th size
8th size
7th size
6th size
5th size
4th size
3rd size
2nd size
1st size

□ colour A
□ colour B

The pattern pieces

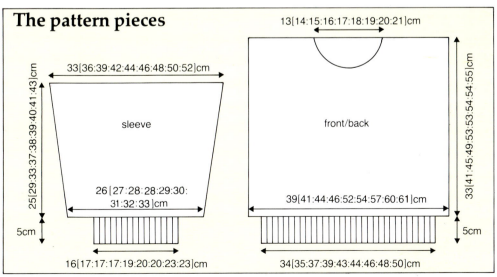

13[14:15:16:17:18:19:20:21]cm

33[36:39:42:44:46:48:50:52]cm

25[29:33:37:38:39:40:41:43]cm

33[41:45:49:53:53:54:54:55]cm

sleeve

front/back

26[27:28:28:29:30:31:32:33]cm

5cm

5cm

16[17:17:17:19:20:20:23:23]cm

39[41:44:46:52:54:57:60:61]cm

34[35:37:39:43:44:46:48:50]cm

Batwing jersey in cool cotton

This striking two-colour batwing design is worked all in one piece, with the ribbed cuffs and neckband picked up and worked afterwards. The neck shaping follows the same line as the stripe, forming a shallow V-shape.

Sizes

To fit 81 [91:102]cm/32 [36:40]in bust
Length to shoulder,
60.5 [61.5:62.5]cm/23¾ [24¼:24¾]in
The figures in [] refer to the 91/36 and 102cm/40in sizes respectively

You will need

11 [12:13]×50g balls Neveda Brenda (78% cotton, 22% viscose) in main shade A
2 balls same in contrast colour B
One pair 2¾mm/No 12 needles
Set of four 2¾mm/No 12 needles
One pair 3¾mm/No 9 needles

Tension

18 sts and 26 rows to 10cm/4in over st st worked on 3¾mm/No 9 needles

Back

With 2¾mm/No 12 needles and A cast on 78 [84:90] sts.
Work 7cm/2¾in K1, P1 rib, ending with a Rs row.

Next row (inc row) Rib 4 [7:10], (inc in next st, rib 14) 5 times, inc in next st, rib 4 [7:10]. 84 [90:96] sts.
Change to 3¾mm/No 9 needles.
Beg with a K row work in st st until back measures 29 [30:31]cm/11½ [11¾:12¼]in, ending with a Ws row.

Shape sleeves

Cast on at the beg of every row 2 sts 40 times, 4 sts 6 times and 16 [17:18] sts twice. 220 [228:236] sts, *at the same time* when there are 104 [110:116] sts commence stripe patt as follows:
1st row Cast on 2 sts, K53 [56:59] A, join in B, K2 B, join in a separate ball of A, K51 [54:57] A.
2nd row Twisting yarns at back of work where colours join to avoid a hole, cast on 2 sts, P52 [55:58] A, P4 B, P52 [55:58] A.
3rd row Cast on 2 sts, K53 [56:59] A, K6 B, K51 [54:57] A.
Cont as set shaping sleeve at beg of every row and working one more st in B each side on every row until there are 40 sts in B.
Next row Cast on 2 sts, K53 [56:59] sts A, K20 B, join in a separate ball of A, K2 A, join in a separate ball of

B, K20 B, K51 [54:57] A.
Working sleeve shaping as given, cont as set working one more st in A each side on every row until there are 40 sts in A in the middle of the row.

Shape neck

Next row Keeping sleeve edges straight, K69 [73:77] A, K20 B, K20 A, turn leaving rem 111 [115:119] sts on holder.
Complete right side of neck first.
Keeping patt correct, dec one st at neck edge for the next 30 rows, ending at neck edge. 79 [83:87] sts.
Mark the last row as top shoulder.
Cont working neck, reversing patt and shaping at neck edge as follows:
Next row In A, inc in first st, P18 A, P20 B, P40 [44:48] A.
Next row K41 [45:49] A, K20 B, K18 A, in A inc in last st.
Cont stripe patt as set moving the stripe back by one st each row and *at the same time* inc one st at neck edge on every row until there are 109 [113:117] sts, ending with a Rs row. Break off yarn and leave sts on a holder.
Return to sts on holder at start of neck shaping.
Next row Join in A, cast off 2 sts, K20 A (incl st on needle), join in B, K20 B, join in a separate ball of A, K to end.
Complete left side of neck to match right, reversing shaping and noting that the marked row at top of shoulder will end at sleeve edge, cont with neck shaping until there are 109 [113:117] sts, ending with a Rs row.

Join left and right sides of neck

Next row P70 [74:78] A, P20 B, P19 A, cast on 2 sts in A, now working across sts on holder from first side of neck, P19 A, P20 B, P70 [74:78] A.
Cont in patt as set for 3 more rows, ending with a Rs row.

Shape sleeves

Keeping patt correct, gradually reducing the colours used, cast off at beg of every row 16 [17:18] sts twice, 4 sts 6 times and 2 sts 40 times. 84 [90:96] sts.
Cont in A only until work measures

The pattern piece

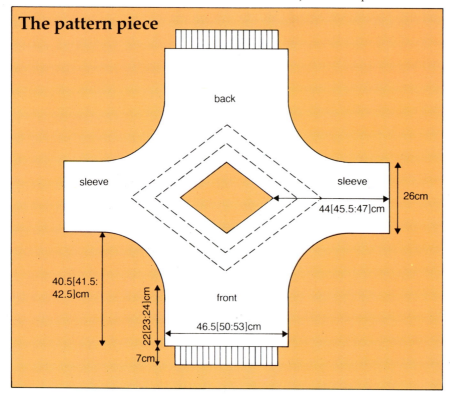

back

sleeve

sleeve

26cm

44[45.5:47]cm

front

40.5[41.5:42.5]cm

22[23:24]cm

46.5[50:53]cm

7cm

same as back to top shoulder marker, ending with a Rs row.

Next row (dec row) P3 [6:9], (P2 tog, P13) 5 times, P2 tog, P4 [7:10]. 78 [84:90] sts.
Change to 2¾mm/No 12 needles.
Work 7cm/2¾in K1, P1 rib.
Cast off in rib.

Cuffs

With Rs of work facing, 2¾mm/No 12 needles and A pick up and K36 sts from sleeve edge.
Work 7cm/2¾in K1, P1 rib.
Cast off loosely in rib.

Neckband

With Rs facing, set of four 2¾mm/No 12 needles and B, *pick up and K30 sts down right side of neck, one st at centre V, 30 sts up left side of neck*, rep from * to * for 2nd side. 122 sts.
Work 3cm/1¼in K1, P1 rib, dec one st either side of centre st at back and front on every row.
Cast off loosely in rib.

To make up

Press lightly with a cool iron.
Join side and sleeve seams.

Right: Stripes from the back and front meet on the shoulder to form a chevron effect. Inset: Close-up of shoulder showing how the stripes match.

Jersey in garter stitch and rib checks

This stylish jersey is knitted in garter stitch and rib checks, and splattered with specks of colour. These are worked by Swiss darning the centre of some of the rib checks, chosen totally at random.

The slash neck is worked in rib which forms a V-shape at the front and back of the jersey and the sleeves are given a lift with shoulder pads.

Below: The Swiss darning can be omitted if you prefer the jersey in one colour only. Inset: Back view of jersey showing the unusual rib V-inset repeated on the back.

Sizes

To fit 86 [91:97]cm/34 [36:38]in bust
Length to shoulder, 61 [62:63]cm/
24 [24½:24¾]in
Sleeve seam, 44cm/17½in
The figures in [] refer to the 91/36
and 97cm/38in sizes respectively

You will need

10 [11:11]×50g balls of Wendy
Fashion Crêpe Double Knitting
(51% Courtelle acrylic, 34% Bri-
nylon, 15% wool) in main colour A
1×50g ball of Wendy Choice Double
Knitting (65% Courtelle acrylic,
20% wool, 15% Bri-nylon) in each
of 3 contrast colours for embroidery
One pair of 3¼mm/No 10 needles
One pair 4mm/No 8 needles
Set of shoulder pads (optional)

Tension

22 sts and 30 rows to 10cm/4in over
st st worked on 4mm/No 8 needles.
26 sts and 30 rows to 10cm/4in over
patt worked on 4mm/No 8 needles

Back

With 3¼mm/No 10 needles and A
cast on 106 [116:126] sts. Work 6cm/
2¼in K1, P1 rib.
Next row (inc row) Rib 8 [4:9] sts,
*pick up loop lying between sts and
K tbl – **called M1**, rib 5 [6:6] sts, rep
from * 17 times more, M1, rib to
end. 125 [135:145] sts.
Change to 4mm/No 8 needles.
Commence patt.
1st row (Rs) K5, *(K1, P1) twice, K6,
rep from * to end.
2nd row K5, *(P1, K1) twice, P1, K5,
rep from * to end.
3rd and 5th rows As 1st.
4th and 6th rows As 2nd.
7th row K1, (P1, K1) twice, *K6, (P1,
K1) twice, rep from * to end.
8th row (P1, K1) twice, *P1, K5, (P1,
K1) twice, rep from * to last st, P1.
9th and 11th rows As 7th.
10th and 12th rows As 8th.
These 12 rows form the patt.
Cont in patt until work measures
39cm/15¼in from beg, ending with
a Ws row.

Shape armholes and work rib inset

Next row Keeping cont of patt
correct, cast off 3 sts, patt 59
[64:69] sts, K1, patt to end.
Next row Cast off 3 sts, patt 59
[64:69] sts, P1, patt to end.
Next row Work 2 tog, patt 57
[62:67] sts, K1, patt 57 [62:67] sts,
work 2 tog.
Next row Work 2 tog, patt 55
[60:65] sts, K1, P1, K1, patt 55
[60:65] sts, work 2 tog.
Next row Work 2 tog, patt 54
[59:64] sts, P1, K1, P1, patt 54
[59:64] sts, work 2 tog.
Next row Work 2 tog, patt 53
[58:63] sts, K1, P1, K1, patt 53
[58:63] sts, work 2 tog.
Next row Work 2 tog, patt 51
[56:61] sts, (K1, P1) twice, K1, patt
51 [56:61] sts, work 2 tog.
Next row Work 2 tog, patt 50
[55:60] sts, (P1, K1) twice, P1, patt
50 [55:60] sts, work 2 tog.
Next row Work 2 tog, patt 49
[54:59] sts, (K1, P1) twice, K1, patt
49 [54:59] sts, work 2 tog.
Next row Work 0 [2:2] tog, patt 49
[52:57] sts, (K1, P1) 3 times, K1, patt
49 [52:57] sts, work 0 [2:2] tog.
Next row Work 2 tog, patt 47
[51:56] sts, (P1, K1) 3 times, P1, patt
47 [51:56] sts, work 2 tog.
Next row Work 0 [0:2] tog, patt 48
[52:55] sts, (K1, P1) 3 times, K1, patt
48 [52:55] sts, work 0 [0:2] tog.
Keeping patt correct throughout,
cont dec one st at each end of every
alt row until 95 [101:105] sts rem, *at
the same time* cont working 2 more
sts in ribbed inset on every 3rd row
as before.
Cont without shaping and work
2 more sts in ribbed inset on every
3rd row until there are 41 [43:45]
inset sts.
Cont in patt and rib as now set until
work measures 22 [23:24]cm/
8¾ [9:9½]in from beg, ending with
a Ws row.

Shape shoulders

Cast off 27 [29:30] sts for shoulder,
cast off 41 [43:45] sts evenly in rib
for neck then cast off rem sts for
other shoulder.

Front

Work as given for back.

Sleeves

With 3¼mm/No 10 needles and A
cast on 42 [44:46] sts. Work 7cm/
2¾in K1, P1 rib.
Next row (inc row) Rib 4 [2:5] sts,
*M1, rib 1 [2:2] sts, M1, rib 2, rep
from * 10 [9:8] times more, M1, rib
to end. 65 sts.
Change to 4mm/No 8 needles. Cont
in patt as given for back, inc one st
at each end of 5th and every foll 5th
row until there are 101 [103:105] sts,
working extra sts into patt.
Cont without shaping until sleeve
measures 44cm/17½in from beg,
ending with a Ws row and same
patt row as on back at beg of
armhole shaping.

Shape top

Keeping patt correct, cast off 3 sts at
beg of next 2 rows. Dec one st at
each end of next and every alt row
until 59 [61:63] sts rem, then at each
end of every row until 33 sts rem.
Cast off.

Embroidery

With Rs of work facing, Swiss darn
6 sts vertically over centre st of each
ribbed check at random on back,
front and sleeves, using colours as
required.

To make up

Do not press. Join shoulder seams.
Set in sleeves. Join side and sleeve
seams. Sew in optional shoulder
pads.

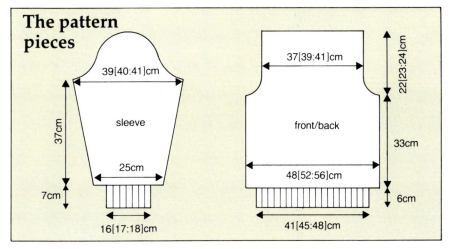

The pattern pieces

sleeve
39[40:41]cm
37cm
25cm
7cm
16[17:18]cm

front/back
37[39:41]cm
22[23:24]cm
33cm
48[52:56]cm
6cm
41[45:48]cm

Lacy slipover

Sizes

To fit 84 [91:99]cm/33 [36:39]in bust
Length to shoulder, 55 [56:57]cm/
21¾ [22:22½]in
The figures in [] refer to the 91/36
and 99cm/39in sizes respectively

You will need

5 [6:6]×50g balls of Sirdar Country
  Style Double Knitting (45% acrylic,
  40% nylon, 15% wool)
One pair 3mm/No 11 needles
One pair 3¾mm/No 9 needles
Set of four 3mm/No 11 needles
One cable needle

Tension

24 sts and 33 rows to 10cm/4in over
st st worked on 3¾mm/No 9 needles

Back

With 3mm/No 11 needles cast on
103 [113:123] sts.
1st row K1, *P1, K1, rep from * to end.
2nd row P1, *K1, P1, rep from * to
end. Rep these 2 rows 15 times more.
Next row (inc row) (K1, P1) twice,
*K3 [4:5] sts, (M1, K3) 3 times, M1,
K3 [4:5] sts, P1, (K1, P1) twice, rep
from * 4 times more omitting last P1
at end of row. 123 [133:143] sts.
Change to 3¾mm/No 9 needles.
1st row (Rs) P1, sl 1 in a purlwise
direction keeping yarn at back of
work – **called sl 1**, P1, *sl 1,
P19 [21:23] sts, (sl 1, P1) twice, rep
from * to end.
2nd row K1, P1, K1, *P1, K19 [21:23]
sts, (P1, K1) twice, rep from * to end.
Rep these 2 rows 3 times more.
9th row P1, sl 1, P1, *sl 1, P5 [6:7] sts,
P2 tog tbl, yon and hold across
needle, sl next st on to cable needle
and hold at back of work, sl 1 from
left-hand needle, yfwd between
needles ready to P1 from cable
needle – **called cr2R**, P1, sl next st
on to cable needle and hold at front
of work, P1, sl 1 from cable needle
(on to right hand needle) – **called
cr2L**, yrn, P2 tog, P5 [6:7] sts, (sl 1,
P1) twice, rep from * to end.
Note: When working cr2R take care
not to lose the st formed by the yon.
10th row K1, P1, K1, *P1, K7 [8:9] sts,
P1, K3, P1, K7 [8:9] sts, (P1, K1)
twice, rep from * to end.
11th row P1, sl 1, P1, *sl 1, P4 [5:6] sts
P2 tog tbl, yon, cr2R, P3, cr2L, yrn,
P2 tog, P4 [5:6] sts, (sl 1, P1) twice,

rep from * to end.
12th row K1, P1, K1, *P1, K6 [7:8] sts,
P1, K5, P1, K6 [7:8] sts, (P1, K1)
twice, rep from * to end.
13th row P1, sl 1, P1, *sl 1, P3 [4:5] sts,
P2 tog tbl, yon, cr2R, P5, cr2L, yrn,
P2 tog, P3 [4:5] sts, (sl 1, P1) twice,
rep from * to end.
14th row K1, P1, K1, *P1, K5 [6:7] sts,
P1, K7, P1, K5 [6:7] sts, (P1, K1)
twice, rep from * to end.
15th row P1, sl 1, P1, *sl 1, P2 [3:4]
sts, P2 tog tbl, yon, cr2R, P1, cr2R, P1,
cr2L, P1, cr2L, yrn, P2 tog, P2 [3:4]
sts, (sl 1, P1) twice, rep from * to end.
16th row K1, P1, K1, *P1, K4 [5:6] sts,
P1, K2, P1, K3, P1, K2, P1, K4 [5:6]
sts, (P1, K1) twice, rep from * to end.
17th row P1, sl 1, P1, *sl 1, P1 [2:3] sts,
P2 tog tbl, yon, cr2R, P1, cr2R, P3,
cr2L, P1, cr2L, yrn, P2 tog, P1 [2:3]
sts, (sl 1, P1) twice, rep from * to end.
18th row K1, P1, K1, *P1, K3 [4:5] sts,
P1, K2, P1, K5, P1, K2, P1, K3 [4:5]
sts, (P1, K1) twice, rep from * to end.
19th row P1, sl 1, P1, *sl 1, P5 [6:7] sts,
cr2R, P5, cr2L, P5 [6:7] sts, (sl 1, P1)
twice, rep from * to end.
20th row K1, P1, K1, *P1, K5 [6:7] sts,
P1, K7, P1, K5 [6:7] sts, (P1, K1)
twice, rep from * to end.
21st row P1, sl 1, Pl, *sl 1, P4 [5:6] sts,
cr2R, P7, cr2L, P4 [5:6] sts, (sl 1, P1)
twice, rep from * to end.
22nd row K1, P1, K1, *P1, K4 [5:6]
sts, P1, K9, P1, K4 [5:6] sts, (P1, K1)
twice, rep from * to end.
23rd row P1, sl 1, P1, *sl 1, P3 [4:5]
sts, cr2R, P9, cr2L, P3 [4:5] sts, (sl 1,
P1) twice, rep from * to end.
24th row K1, P1, K1, *P1, K3 [4:5] sts,
P1, K11, Pl, K3 [4:5] sts, (P1, K1)
twice, rep from * to end.
These 24 rows form patt and are rep
throughout. Cont in patt until work
measures 33cm/13in from beg,
ending with a Ws row.

Shape armholes

Cast off at beg of next and every row
4 [5:6] sts twice, 3 sts 4 times, 2 sts 8
times and one st 4 [6:8] times. 83
[89:95] sts. Work 6 [8:10] rows
without shaping.
Inc one st at each end of next and
every foll 6th row until there are 99
[105:111] sts. Cont without shaping
until armholes measure 22 [23:24]cm/
8¾ [9:9½]in from beg, ending with
a Ws row.

Shape shoulders and neck

Cast off 5 sts at beg of next 4 rows.

Next row Cast off 5 sts, patt 18 [20:22]
sts, turn and leave rem sts on holder.
Complete right side first.
Cast off at beg of next and every row
4 sts once, 5 [6:7] sts once, 4 sts once
and 5 [6:7] sts once.
With Rs of work facing sl next 33
[35:37] sts on to holder for centre
neck, rejoin yarn to rem sts and patt
to end. Complete to match first side
reversing shaping.

Front

Work as given for back until point
where you have inc to 93 [99:105] sts
in armhole shaping, ending with a
Ws row.

Shape neck

Next row Patt 39 [41:43] sts, turn and
leave rem sts on holder.
Cont inc at armhole edge on every
6th row 3 times more, *at the same time*
cast off at neck edge on next and
every alt row 3 sts once, 2 sts 3 times
and one st 8 times. Cont without
shaping until armhole measures
same as back to shoulder, ending
with a Ws row.

Shape shoulder

Cast off at beg of next and every alt
row 5 sts 3 times and 5 [6:7] sts twice.
With Rs of work facing sl next 15
[17:19] sts on to holder for centre
neck, rejoin yarn to rem sts and patt
to end. Complete to match first side
reversing shaping.

Neckband

Join shoulder seams. With four 3mm/
No 11 needles and Rs facing, pick up
and K9 sts down right back neck, K
across back neck sts, pick up and K9
sts up left back neck and 26 sts down
left front neck, K across front neck
sts, pick up and K26 sts up right front
neck. 118 [122:126] sts.
Work 8 rounds K1, P1 rib. Cast off
loosely in rib.

Armbands

With 3mm/No 11 needles and Rs
facing, pick up and K103 [109:115]
sts round armhole. Beg with 2nd rib
row, work 6 rows rib as for back,
dec one st at each end of 2nd and
every alt row. Cast off in rib.

To make up

Press each piece under a dry cloth
with a warm iron, omitting ribbing.
Join side seams. Press seams.

Double-breasted waistcoat

This low-buttoning waistcoat is knitted in a wool and silk mixture, in simple basket stitch and moss stitch. The buttonholes are worked vertically in pairs. Six sizes are given to include larger measurements.

Sizes

To fit 86[91:97:102:107:112]cm/ 34[36:38:40:42:44]in bust
Length to shoulder, 56[57:58:60:61:62]cm/ 22[22½:23:23½:24:24½]in
The figures in [] refer to the 91/36, 97/38, 102/40, 107/42 and 112cm/44in sizes respectively

You will need

11[12:12:13:13:14]×20g balls of Jaeger Wool/Silk (60% wool, 40% silk)
One pair 2¾mm/No 12 needles
One pair 3¼mm/No 10 needles
Four buttons

Tension

28 sts and 36 rows to 10cm/4in over st st worked on 3¼mm/No 10 needles

Below: The stitches are decreased for the moss stitch yoke of this waistcoat to allow for the different tensions.

Back

With 2¾mm/No 12 needles cast on 115[123:129:137:145:151] sts.
1st row (Rs) K1, *P1, K1, rep from * to end.
2nd row P1, *K1, P1, rep from * to end.
Rep these 2 rows 16 times more then first row again.
Next row (Ws) Rib 10[4:7:5:6:13] sts, pick up loop lying between needles and K tbl – **called M1**, (rib 5[5:5:6:7:5] sts, M1) 19[23:23:21:19:25] times, rib to end. 135[147:153:159:165:177] sts.
Change to 3¼mm/No 10 needles.
Commence patt.
1st row (Rs) K3, *P3, K3, rep from * to end.
2nd row P3, *K3, P3, rep from * to end.
3rd and 4th rows As 1st and 2nd.
5th row P3, *K3, P3, rep from * to end.
6th row K3, *P3, K3, rep from * to end.
7th and 8th rows As 5th and 6th.
These 8 rows form the patt. Cont in patt until work measures 34cm/13½in from beg, ending with an 8th row.

Shape armholes

Keeping patt correct, cast off 9 sts at beg of next 2 rows.
Work 14 rows without shaping, ending with an 8th row.
Next row (dec row) K8[9:8:6:5:6] sts, *K2 tog, K9[10:11:12:13:14] sts, rep from * 8 times more, K2 tog, K8[10:8:7:5:7] sts.
107[119:125:131:137:149] sts.
Commence moss st patt.
Next row K1, *P1, K1, rep from * to end.

Left: Close-up showing the small vertical buttonholes worked into the welt of the waistcoat.

Rep this row until work measures 22[23:24:26:27:28]cm/8¾[9:9½:10¼:10¾:11]in from cast off sts at armholes, ending with a Ws row.

Shape shoulders

Cast off at beg of next and every row 8[9:9:10:10:11] sts 6 times and 7[9:10:9:10:12] sts twice.
Cast off rem 45[47:51:53:57:59] sts.

Left front

With 2¾mm/No 12 needles cast on 77[79:83:87:91:95] sts.
Work 35 rows rib as given for back.
Next row (inc row) Rib 7[5:6:5:7:7] sts, M1, (rib 7[10:8:7:11:9] sts, M1) 9[7:9:11:7:9] times, rib to end. 87[87:93:99:99:105] sts.
Change to 3¼mm/No 10 needles.
Work 8 rows patt as given for back.

Shape front edge

Keeping patt correct throughout, dec one st at end of next and at same edge on every foll 3rd row until 60[60:66:72:72:78] sts rem. Work one row, ending with a Ws row.

Shape armhole

Cast off 9 sts, patt to end.
Cont to dec one st at front edge as before on every 3rd row until 46[46:52:58:58:64] sts rem. Work 2 rows ending with an 8th patt row.
Next row (dec row) K4[4:5:6:6:7] sts, *K2 tog, K7[7:8:9:9:10] sts, rep from * 3 times more, K2 tog, K2[2:3:4:4:5] sts, K2 tog. 40[40:46:52:52:58] sts.
Cont in moss st patt, cont to dec one st at front edge on every foll 4th row until 31[36:37:39:40:45] sts rem.
Cont without shaping until work measures same as back to shoulder, ending at armhole edge.

Shape shoulder

Cast off at beg of next and every alt row 8[9:9:10:10:11] sts 3 times and 7[9:10:9:10:12] sts once.

Right front

With 2¾mm/No 12 needles cast on 77[79:83:87:91:95] sts. Work 6 rows rib as given for back.
**Next row Rib 6 sts, turn.
Work 3 rows rib on these 6 sts.
Leave sts on safety pin.

With Rs facing and another ball of yarn, rejoin yarn to rem sts and rib 12 sts, turn.
Work 3 rows rib on these 12 sts.
Leave sts on safety pin. Break off yarn.
With Rs facing rejoin yarn to rem sts and rib to end. Work 3 rows rib on these sts. Break off yarn.
With Rs of work facing rib across first 6 sts on safety pin, then 12 sts on safety pin, rib to end.**. Work 15 rows rib across all sts.
Rep from ** to ** once more.
Work 4 rows rib across all sts.
Work inc row as given for left front and complete to match left front, reversing all shapings.

Front borders (make 2)

Join shoulder seams. With 2¾mm/No 12 needles cast on 21 sts.
1st row (Rs) K2, *P1, K1, rep from * to last st, K1.
2nd row K1, *P1, K1, rep from * to end.
Rep these 2 rows until border, when slightly stretched, fits up front neck to centre back neck, sewing in position as you go.

Armhole borders

Work as given for front borders until borders, when slightly stretched, fit round armhole, sewing in position as you go.

To make up

Do not press. Join front borders at centre back neck. Fold front border in half to Ws and sl st down. Join side seams. Fold armhole borders in half to Ws and sl st down. Neaten at armhole shaping. Sew on buttons.

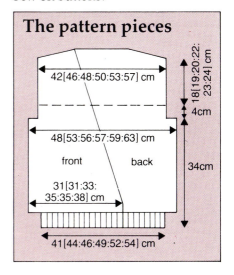

The pattern pieces

42[46:48:50:53:57] cm
18[19:20:22:23:24] cm
4cm
48[53:56:57:59:63] cm
front   back
34cm
31[31:33:35:35:38] cm
41[44:46:49:52:54] cm

Cardigan or jersey with wavy stripes

Choose to make either a cardigan or jersey in these contrasting textured yarns produced in a colour range specially to complement each other. The simple pattern forms a wave effect which is accentuated by the narrow stripes worked in the random bouclé yarn. Both the jersey and cardigan have short sleeves, and all the borders are worked in single rib.

Sizes

To fit 86–91 [91–96]cm/34–36 [36–38]in bust
Length to shoulders, 58 [60]cm/22¾ [23½]in
Sleeve seam, 9cm/3½in
The figures in [] refer to the 91–96cm/36–38in size only

You will need

Cardigan 4 [5]×50g balls of Wendy Dolce (50% Courtelle acrylic, 50% Bri-nylon) in main colour A
1×50g ball of Wendy Donna (77% Courtelle acrylic, 15% mohair, 6% polyester, 2% Bri-nylon) in contrast colour B
Seven buttons
Jersey 4 [5]×50g balls of Wendy Dolce in main colour A
1×50g ball of Wendy Donna in contrast colour B
One pair 3¼mm/No 10 needles
One pair 4mm/No 8 needles

Tension

25 sts and 26 rows to 10cm/4in over patt worked on 4mm/No 8 needles

Cardigan back

With 3¼mm/No 10 needles and A cast on 97 [113] sts.
1st row K1, *P1, K1, rep from * to end.
2nd row P1, *K1, P1, rep from * to end.
Rep these 2 rows until work measures 6cm/2¼in from beg, ending with a 1st row.
Next row (inc row) Rib 4, inc in next st, (rib 5 [7], inc in next st) 15 [13] times, rib 2 [4]. 113 [127] sts.
Change to 4mm/No 8 needles.

Left: The cardigan, worked in soft toning colours, can either be worn open over a blouse as a waistcoat or buttoned up on its own.

Commence patt.
1st row With A, K to end.
2nd row P to end.
3rd row K1, *yfwd, K5, sl 1, K2 tog, psso, K5, yfwd, K1, rep from * to end.
4th row P to end.
Rep 3rd and 4th rows 3 times more.
11th row With B, K to end.
12th row With B, K to end.
These 12 rows form patt, rep until back measures 33cm/13in from beg, ending with a 12th patt row.

Shape sleeves

Cast on 14 sts at beg of next 2 rows. 141 [155] sts.
Keeping patt correct, cont without shaping until sleeve edge measures 25 [27]cm/9¾ [10¾]in from beg, ending with a 6th patt row.
Cast off.

Cardigan left front

With 3¼mm/No 10 needles and A cast on 49 [53] sts.
Work 6cm/2¼in rib as given for back, ending with a 1st row.
Next row (inc row) Rib 4 [6], inc in next st, (rib 5 [4], inc in next st) 7 [9] times, rib 2 [1]. 57 [63] sts.**
Change to 4mm/No 8 needles.
Commence patt.
1st row With A, K to end.
2nd row P to end.
3rd row K1, *yfwd, K5, sl 1, K2 tog, psso, K5, yfwd, K1, rep from * to last 0 [6] sts, K0 [yfwd, K4, K2 tog].
4th row P to end.
Rep 3rd and 4th rows 3 times more.
11th row With B, K to end.

12th row With B, K to end.
These 12 rows form patt, rep until front measures 33cm/13in from beg, ending with a 12th patt row.

Shape sleeve

Cast on 14 sts at beg of next row. 71 [77] sts.
Keeping patt correct, cont without shaping until sleeve edge measures 15 [16]cm/6 [6¼]in, ending at neck edge.

Shape neck

Keeping patt correct, K the first 6 [7] sts and sl on to a safety pin, patt to end of row.
Dec one st at neck edge on every foll row 6 [8] times, then every foll alt row 4 times. 55 [58] sts.
Cont in patt until front measures same as back to shoulder, ending with a 6th patt row.
Cast off.

Cardigan right front

Work as given for left front to **
Change to 4mm/No 8 needles.
Commence patt.
1st row With A, K to end.
2nd row P to end.
3rd row K1, [K2 tog, K4, yfwd, K1], * yfwd, K5, sl 1, K2 tog, psso, K5, yfwd, K1, rep from * to end.
4th row P to end.
Rep 3rd and 4th rows 3 times more.
11th row With B, K to end.
12th row With B, K to end.
Cont in patt and complete right front to match left front, reversing all shaping.

The pattern pieces

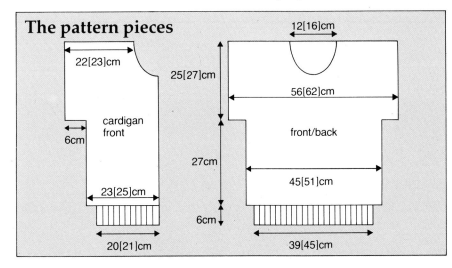

22[23]cm
25[27]cm
6cm
cardigan front
23[25]cm
20[21]cm

12[16]cm
56[62]cm
front/back
27cm
6cm
45[51]cm
39[45]cm

safety pin, then rib across 11 sts from button band. 99 [105] sts.
Work 12 rows in rib working a buttonhole as before on the 2nd row at the right front.
Cast off loosely in rib.

Jersey back

Work as given for cardigan back.

Jersey front

Work as given for cardigan back to the start of sleeve shaping.

Shape sleeves

Cast on 14 sts at beg of next 2 rows. 141 [155] sts.
Keeping patt correct, cont without shaping until sleeve edge measures 15 [16]cm/6 [6¼]in, ending with a Ws row.

Shape neck

Patt across 65 [70] sts, turn and leave rem sts on holder.
Complete left shoulder first.
Dec one st at neck edge on next and every foll row 6 [8] times, then every foll alt row twice. 57 [58] sts.
Cont in patt until front measures same as back to shoulder, ending with a 6th patt row.
Cast off.
Leave the first 11 [15] of rem sts on holder, rejoin yarn and patt to end.
Complete right shoulder to match left shoulder, reversing all shaping.

Neckband

Join right shoulder seam.
With Rs of work facing, 3¼mm/ No 10 needles and A pick up and K24 [25] sts down left side of neck, K across 11 [15] sts on front neck holder, pick up and K24 [25] sts up right side of neck and 37 [39] sts along back neck. 96 [104] sts.
Work 12 rows in K1, P1 rib.
Cast off loosely in rib.

Sleeve edges

Join left shoulder and neckband seam.
With Rs of work facing, 3¼mm/ No 10 needles and A pick up and K96 [100] sts evenly along sleeve edge.
Work 3cm/1¼in K1, P1 rib.
Cast off loosely in rib.

To make up

Do not press. Join side seams. Sew buttons on to cardigan version.

Sleeve edges

Join shoulder seams.
With Rs of work facing, 3¼mm/ No 10 needles and A pick up and K96 [100] sts evenly along sleeve edge.
Work 3cm/1¼in K1, P1 rib.
Cast off loosely in rib.

Button band

With 3¼mm/No 10 needles and A cast on 11 sts.
Work in K1, P1 rib as given for back, beg with a 2nd row, until band is long enough to fit front edge when slightly stretched.
Leave sts on holder for neckband.

Buttonhole band

Cast on as given for button band and work 4 [6] rows in rib.
Next row (buttonhole row) Rib 4, cast off 3 sts, rib to end.

Above: Also worked in toning colours, the jersey version of this pattern has a round neck and short sleeves.

Next rib Rib to end casting on 3 sts above those cast off in previous row.
Work 20 rows in rib.
Rep the last 22 rows 4 times more, then the 2 buttonhole rows once more.
Work 18 [20] rows in rib.
Leave sts on holder for neckband.

Neckband

With Rs of work facing, 3¼mm/ No 10 needles and A rib across the 11 sts of buttonhole band, K across 6 [7] sts from safety pin on right front neck, pick up and K16 [17]sts up right side of neck, 33 [35] sts from back neck, 16 [17] sts down left side of neck, K across 6 [7] sts from

Sparkling party top for evening

This dazzling evening top is decorated with bands of shimmering sequins knitted in at the waistline and on the sleeves. Thread multiples of sequins straight from the hanks on to the yarn using a needle. The main area of the top is worked in stocking stitch.

Sizes
To fit 86-97cm/34-38in bust loosely
Length to shoulder, 39cm/15¼in

You will need
3×50g balls of Pingouin Oued (80% acrylic, 10% wool, 10% mohair)
One pair 3mm/No 11 needles
One pair 3¾mm/No 9 needles
3×10mm/½in hanks of sequins

Tension
24 sts and 36 rows to 10cm/4in over st st worked on 3¾mm/No 9 needles

Note
Thread one ball of yarn with sequins before beginning to knit

Back
With 3mm/No 11 needles and plain yarn cast on 131 sts.
Beg with a K row work 5 rows st st.
Next row (hemline) K all sts tbl. Break off plain yarn and join in yarn threaded with sequins. Change to 3¾mm/No 9 needles. Commence border patt.
1st row (Rs) *K1, put needle into next st knitwise, push sequin up close to back of work and push sequin through st to front then K st in usual way to secure sequin – **called sequin 1**, rep from * to last st, K1.
2nd and 4th rows P to end.
3rd row K1, *K1, sequin 1, rep from * to last 2 sts, K2.
Rep these 4 rows of border patt 3 times more. Break off yarn threaded with sequins and join in plain yarn.
Beg with a K row cont in st st until work measures 39cm/15¼in from hemline, ending with a Rs row.

Shape neck and shoulders
Next row Cast off 34 sts at beg of row, P to end.
Next row (foldline) Cast off 34 sts at beg of row, P to end.
Change to 3mm/No 11 needles.
Beg with a K row work 4 rows st st, inc one st at each end of every row for folded-under neck edge. Cast off.

Front
Work as given for back.

Armbands
With 3mm/No 11 needles and plain yarn cast on 119 sts.
Beg with a K row work 3 rows st st.
Next row (hemline) K all sts tbl. Break off plain yarn and join in yarn threaded with sequins.
Change to 3¾mm/No 9 needles.
Rep 4 rows of border patt as

Above: The neckline of this attractive top is neatened with a stocking stitch facing.

given for back 4 times. Break off yarn threaded with sequins and join in plain yarn.
Beg with a K row work 2 rows st st. Cast off

To make up
Do not press. Join shoulder seams.
Join points of folded-under neck edge, turn to Ws at foldline and sl st in place.
With cast off edge at armhole, place centre of armband to shoulder seam and sew in place round armhole so that only sequin patt shows. Join lower edge of armbands with flat seam. Join side seams. Turn hems at lower edge and on armbands to Ws and sl st in place.

Mohair cardigan with pierrot collar

Knit this lovely mohair cardigan to wear on cool summer evenings or for extra warmth in winter.
Choose from a pretty pierrot-style collar, or use the plain rib neckband.

Sizes

To fit 81 [86:91]cm/32 [34:36]in bust
Length to shoulder, 49 [51:53]cm/ 19¼ [20:20¾]in, adjustable
Sleeve seam, 42cm/16½in, adjustable
The figures in [] refer to the 86/34 and 91cm/36in sizes respectively

You will need

7 [7:8]×40g balls of Pingouin Mohair (85% mohair, 15% nylon)
One pair 4mm/No 8 needles
One pair 5mm/No 6 needles
Seven small buttons

Tension

17 sts and 22 rows to 10cm/4in over reversed st st worked on 5mm/No 6 needles

Back

With 4mm/No 8 needles cast on 72 [76:80] sts.
1st row (Rs) K1, *P2, K2, rep from * to last 3 sts, P2, K1.
2nd row P1, *K2, P2, rep from * to last 3 sts, K2, P1.
Rep these 2 rows 9 times more.
Change to 5mm/No 6 needles.
Beg with a P row cont in reversed st st until work measures 32 [33:34]cm/ 12½ [13:13½]in from beg, or required length to underarm, ending with a K row.

Shape armholes

Cast off at beg of next and every row 5 sts twice and 3 sts twice.
Dec one st at each end of next and foll alt row. 52 [56:60] sts.
Cont without shaping until armholes measure 15 [16:17]cm/6 [6¼: 6¾]in from beg, or required length to back neck ending with a K row.

Shape neck

Next row P21 [23:25] sts, cast off 10 sts for centre back neck, P21 [23:25] sts.
Complete left shoulder first.
Dec one st at neck edge on every row until 16 [18:20] sts rem, ending at armhole edge.

Shape shoulder

Cast off 8 [9:10] sts at beg of next and foll alt row.
With Ws of work facing, rejoin yarn to rem sts and complete right shoulder to match left side.

Right front

With 4mm/No 8 needles cast on 44 [44:48] sts. Work 6 rows rib as given for back.
Next row (buttonhole row) Rib 4 sts, cast off one st, rib to end.
Next row Rib to end casting on one above st cast off in previous row.
Work 12 more rows ribbing, inc one st in each of first 2 sts of last row on 2nd size only. 44 [46:48] sts.
Next row Rib 8 sts, leave these sts on safety pin for front band, change to 5mm/No 6 needles, P to end. 36 [38:40] sts.
Cont in reversed st st until work measures same as back to underarm, ending at armhole edge.

Shape armhole

Cast off at beg of next and foll alt row 5 sts once and 3 sts once. Dec one st at same edge on foll 2 alt rows. 26 [28:30] sts.
Work 22 [24:26] rows without shaping, ending at neck edge.

Shape neck

Cast off at beg of next and foll alt row 5 sts once and 3 sts once. Dec one st at neck edge on every row until 16 [18:20] sts rem.
Cont without shaping until armhole measures same as back to shoulder, ending at armhole edge.

Shape shoulder

Cast off at beg of next and foll alt row 8 [9:10] sts twice.

Left front

Work as given for right front, omitting buttonhole and reversing all shapings.

Right: This cardigan is worked in reverse stocking stitch with knit-two, purl-two ribbing. The fluted effect collar is edged with garter stitch.

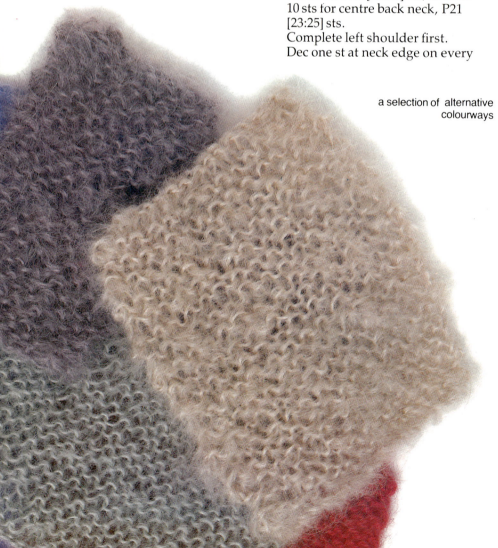

a selection of alternative colourways

Above: Close up showing the alternative ribbed neckband.

Sleeves

With 4mm/No 8 needles cast on 40 [44:44] sts. Work 12 rows rib as given for back, inc one st at each end of last row. 42 [46:46] sts. Change to 5mm/No 6 needles. Beg with a P row cont in reversed st st, inc one st at each end of 7th and every foll 8th row until there are 54 [58:62] sts.
Cont without shaping until sleeve measures 42cm/16½in from beg, or required length to underarm, ending with a K row.

Shape top

Cast off 5 sts at beg of next 2 rows. Work 10 rows without shaping. Dec one st at each end of next and every foll alt row until 20 [24:28] sts

rem. Cast off 4 sts at beg of next 2 rows. Cast off rem sts.

Button band

With 4mm/No 8 needles, rejoin yarn to inner edge of sts left on safety pin for left front.
Cont in rib until band, when slightly stretched, fits up front edge to beg of neck shaping. Cast off in rib. Mark positions for 7 buttons on front edge, first to come level with buttonhole already worked and last to come about 1cm/½in below beg of neck shaping, with 5 more evenly spaced between.

Buttonhole band

With 4mm/No 8 needles, rejoin yarn to inner edge of sts left on safety pin for right front.
Cont in rib, making buttonholes as given as markers are reached, until

band when slightly stretched fits up front edge to beginning of neck shaping.
Cast off in rib.

Neckband for collar

Join shoulder seams. With Rs of work facing and 4mm/No 8 needles, pick up and K18 sts up right front neck, 24 sts across back neck and 18 sts down left front neck. 60 sts.
K 3 rows g st. Cast off knitwise.

Collar

With 4mm/No 8 needles cast on 108 sts.
Work 6cm/2¼in rib as given for back.
Next row Cast on 8 sts for side edge of collar, K across these 8 sts, K twice into each of next 108 sts, turn and cast on 8 sts for other side edge of collar. 232 sts.
K 3 rows g st. Cast off knitwise.

Ribbed neckband

(alternative to collar)
Join shoulder seams.
With Rs of work facing and 4mm/No 8 needles pick up and K sts round neck as given for neckband for collar. 60 sts.
Work 8 rows rib as given for back. Cast off in rib.

To make up

Do not press.
Sew in sleeves. Join side and sleeve seams. Sew on front bands. Sew on buttons.
Cardigan with collar Sew collar to neck edge, sewing the 8 cast-on sts at each end to side edges of collar on the reverse side.

The pattern pieces

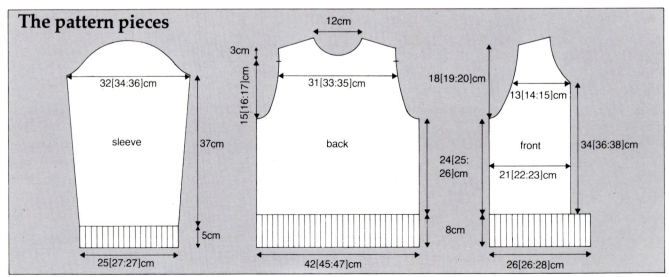

Soft, pretty jersey with flower motif

This jersey has the stylish thirties look. A mock ribbed opening is picked up in a line across the front of the work and the neck edge is finished with a padded flower motif. The main fabric of the body and sleeves has a tiny bobble worked at intervals to add texture to the soft, lightweight yarn.

Sizes

To fit 86 [91:97]cm/34 [36:38]in bust
Length to shoulder, 61 [63:65]cm/24 [24¾:25½]in
Sleeve seam, 45.5cm/18in with cuff turned back
The figures in [] refer to the 91/36 and 97cm/38in sizes respectively

You will need

7 [8:8]×50g balls of Phildar Dedicace (75% acrylic, 20% mohair, 5% wool) in main colour A
1 [1:1] ball each of same in contrast colours B, C and D
One pair 2¾mm/No 12 needles
One pair 3¾mm/No 9 needles
One 2¾mm/No 12 circular needle 40cm/16in long
Small piece of lining material to match colour A
Small amount of wadding as backing for flower motif
Three small buttons

Tension

24 sts and 32 rows to 10cm/4in over st st worked on 3¾mm/No 9 needles

Back

With 2¾mm/No 12 needles and B cast on 101 [107:113] sts.
1st row (Rs) With B, K2, *P1, K1, rep from * to last st, K1.
2nd row With A, K1, *P1, K1, rep from * to end.
3rd row With A, as 1st.
Rep the 2nd and 3rd rows until work measures 6cm/2¼in from beg, ending with a 3rd row.
Next row (inc row) Rib 1 [4:2] sts, *rib 4 [4:5] sts, inc in next st, rib 5 sts, rep from * to last 0 [3:1] sts, rib to end. 111 [117:123] sts.
Change to 3¾mm/No 9 needles.
Cont in A, beg with a K row work 4 rows st st.
Commence bobble patt.
1st row (Rs) K2, *K5, P into front then into back of next st, turn and K2, turn and sl 1, K1, psso – **called MB**, rep from * to last 7 sts, K7.
2nd row P to end.
Beg with a K row work 6 rows st st.
9th row K2, *K2, MB, K3, rep from * to last st, K1.
10th row As 2nd.
Beg with a K row work 6 rows st st. These 16 rows form the patt. Cont in patt until work measures 39 [40:41]cm/15¼ [15¾:16¼]in from beg, ending with a Ws row.

Shape armholes

Cast off 8 sts at beg of next 2 rows. 95 [101:107] sts.
Cont in patt without shaping until armholes measure 22 [23:24]cm/8¾ [9:9½]in from beg, ending with a Ws row.

Shape shoulders

Cast off 15 [16:17] sts at beg of next 4 rows.
Cast off rem 35 [37:39] sts for centre back neck loosely.

Front

Work as given for back until armholes measure 1 [2:3]cm/½ [¾: 1¼]in from beg, ending with a Ws row.
Commence flower motif.
Next row With A, patt 44 [47:50] sts, with C, K4, with 2nd ball of A, patt rem 47 [50:53] sts.
Keeping patt in A on each side of flower motif correct, beg with 2nd row and work flower motif from chart in st st only, omitting bobbles, until 42 rows have been completed.

Shape front neck

Next row Patt across first 47 [50: 53] sts, K2 tog, patt across rem 46 [49:52] sts.
Complete right shoulder first, on last set of sts.
Keep patt correct as now set and when flower motif has been completed, cont with A only.
**Next row Patt 45 [48:51] sts, P2 tog, turn.
Next row Cast off 2 sts, patt to end.
Rep last 2 rows 3 times more.
Next row Patt to last 2 sts, P2 tog.
Next row K2 tog, patt to end.
Rep last 2 rows once more.
Next row Patt to end.
Next row K2 tog, patt to end.
Rep last 2 rows 0 [1:2] times more. 30 [32:34] sts.
Cont in patt without shaping until armhole measures same as back to shoulder, ending at armhole edge.

Shape shoulder

Cast off 15 [16:17] sts at beg of next and foll alt row. ******
With Ws of work facing, rejoin A to rem sts and patt to end.
Work as given for first side from ****** to ******.

Sleeves

With 2¾mm/No 12 needles and B, cast on 41 [47:53] sts. Work 1st row in rib as given for back. Join in A and work 2nd and 3rd rows in rib as given for back until sleeve measures 10cm/4in from beg, ending with a 3rd row.
Next row (inc row) Rib 0 [3:1] sts,

Left: A flower motif makes a striking focal point at the neckline of this simple design. You can omit this if preferred, and work the body in one colour, using a contrast for the edges.

Chart for flower motif

centre of motif

42nd row

A C D

1st row

*rib 2 sts, inc in next st, rib 1 [1:2] sts, rep from * to last 1 [4:2] sts, rib to end. 51 [57:63] sts.
Change to 3¾mm/No 9 needles.
Beg with a K row work 4 rows st st.
Cont in patt as given for back, inc one st at each end of next and every foll 4th row until there are 109 [113:119] sts.
Cont in patt without shaping until sleeve measures 50.5cm/19¾in from beg, allowing for cuff to be turned back, ending with a Ws row.
Place coloured marker at each end of last row.
Work a further 10 rows in patt noting that these rows are set into armhole.

Shape top

Cast off at beg of next and every row 15 sts 6 times and 19 [23:29] sts once.

Above: The flower motif is knitted in with the main fabric and the shape of the petals outlined with embroidery.

Front band

With Rs of work facing, beg at right-hand edge and count along rib sts to the 54th [56th:58th] st and mark this st with coloured thread.
Tack a line from this point diagonally across front to join at outside edge of flower motif. With A, work a line of embroidery ch sts along this tacking line.
With Rs of work facing, 2¾mm/No 12 needles and A, pick up and K 129 [133:137] sts along left-hand side of ch sts.
Beg with a 2nd row work 4 rows rib as given for back, inc one st at neck edge on 2nd and 4th rows.
Join in B and rib one row, then cast off with B in rib.

Neckband

Join shoulder seams.
Work a line of embroidery ch st as given for front band from point of flower motif to centre V of neck.
With Rs of work facing, 2¾mm/No 12 circular needle and A, beg at point of motif, pick up and K51 [53:55] sts along ch st line from point and edge of neck to shoulder, 45 [47:49] sts across back neck and 33 [35:37] sts from shoulder to centre of front neck. 129 [135:141] sts.
Work in rows and complete as given for front band.

Armbands (make two)

With 2¾mm/No 12 needles and B, cast on 119 [123:127] sts. Work 2 rows rib as given for back. Cast off loosely in rib.

To make up

Do not press. Sew in sleeves, folding the armband in half and inserting it between the pieces and sewing last 10 rows of sleeves to cast-off sts at underarms. Join first 5cm/2in of cuff on Rs, then join rem of sleeve seam on Ws. Join side seams. Sew edges of front and neckband tog. Sew on buttons as shown.
Cut lining to shape of flower motif, allowing about 1cm/½in for turning under. Cut wadding to exact shape of flower motif. Place wadding to Ws of lining, turn in edges and catch down. Place wadding on inside of garment under flower motif and invisibly sew in place. With colour B, work embroidery ch st line around both lines of colour C on motif.

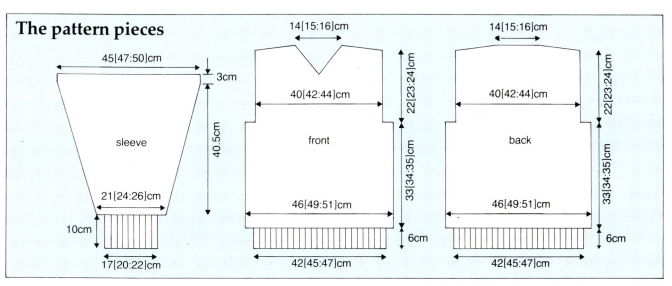

The pattern pieces

sleeve
45[47:50]cm
3cm
40.5cm
21[24:26]cm
10cm
17[20:22]cm

front
14[15:16]cm
40[42:44]cm
22[23:24]cm
33[34:35]cm
46[49:51]cm
6cm
42[45:47]cm

back
14[15:16]cm
40[42:44]cm
22[23:24]cm
33[34:35]cm
46[49:51]cm
6cm
42[45:47]cm

Entrelac jersey in mohair

Knit this stylish jersey in the subtle colours as shown or in bold contrasting colours; it can even be knitted in just one colour if preferred.

The unusual fabric looks as if strips of knitting have been woven in and out to form the trellis pattern but it is knitted all in one piece. Once started, it is an interesting and fascinating design to knit.

Sizes

To fit 81–86 [91–96]cm/
32–34 [36–38]in bust
Length to shoulders, 58cm/22¾in
Sleeve seam, 46cm/18in
The figures in [] refer to the
91–96cm/36–38in size only

You will need

11 [11]×25g balls of Wendy Mohair
 (67% mohair, 28% wool,
 5% nylon) in main colour A
9 [9] balls of same in contrast
 colour B
One pair 3¾mm/No 9 needles
One pair 4½mm/No 7 needles

Tension

16 sts and 22 rows to 10cm/4in over st st worked on 4½mm/No 7 needles

Back

With 3¾mm/No 9 needles and A cast on 82 [94] sts.
Work 5cm/2in K1, P1 rib, ending with a Ws row.
Next row (dec row) Rib 7 [9], *rib 2 tog, rep from * to last 7 [9] sts, rib to end. 48 [56] sts.
Break off A. Change to 4½mm/No 7

Left: Once past the first row of triangles you will see the fabric starting to form the entrelac pattern.

needles. Join in B.
Commence row of 6 [7] base triangles.
1st row (Ws) P2, turn.
2nd row K2, turn.
3rd row P3 (purling one more st from left-hand needle), turn.
4th row K3, turn.
5th row P4 (purling one more st from left-hand needle), turn.
6th row K4, turn.
Cont as now set purling one more st each time until the 12th row has been knitted and 7 sts have been worked in colour B.
13th row P8.
The first base triangle is now complete, do not turn or break off yarn.
Rep the 1st to 13th rows 5 [6] times more. Break off B.
See diagram showing first row of base triangles complete.
*Join in A. Commence selvedge triangle.
1st row K2, turn.
2nd row P2, turn.
3rd row Inc in first st, sl 1, K1, psso, turn.
4th row P3, turn.
5th row Inc in first st, K1, sl 1, K1, psso, turn.
6th row P4, turn.
7th row Inc in first st, K2, sl 1, K1, psso, turn.
8th row P5, turn.
9th row Inc in first st, K3, sl 1, K1, psso, turn.
10th row P6, turn.
11th row Inc in first st, K4, sl 1, K1, psso, turn.
12th row P7, turn.
13th row Inc in first st, K5, sl 1, K1, psso, *do not turn.*
Commence first rectangle.
***1st row** Still with A pick up and

K8 sts along 2nd side of first triangle, turn. See diagram showing stitches picked up for first rectangle.
2nd row P8, turn.
3rd row K7, sl 1, K next st of colour B from left-hand needle, psso, turn.
4th row P8, turn.
Rep last 2 rows until all sts of colour B from the next triangle have been knitted, ending with a K row.**
Rep from ** to ** along each of the next 4 [5] triangles.
Still with A pick up and K8 sts along 2nd side of last triangle, turn.
Commence end selvedge triangle.
1st row P2 tog, P6, turn.
2nd row K7.
3rd row P2 tog, P5, turn.
4th row K6.
5th row P2 tog, P4, turn.
6th row K5.
7th row P2 tog, P3, turn.
8th row K4.
9th row P2 tog, P2, turn.
10th row K3.
11th row P2 tog, P1, turn.
12th row K2.
13th row P2 tog. *Do not turn.*
Break off A, join in B. Commence next row of rectangles.
With one st already on right-hand needle, pick up and P7 sts along straight edge of triangle just completed, turn.
***Next row** K8, turn.
Next row P7, P tog the last of the sts in colour B with the first of the next 8 sts on left-hand needle in colour A, turn.

knitting first row of base triangles

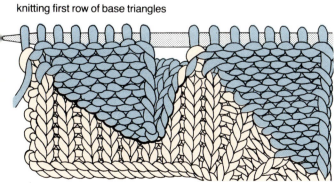

picking up stitches for first rectangle

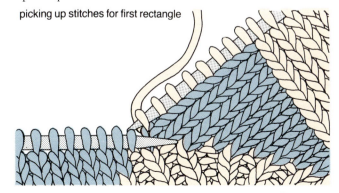

Above: The slit neckline is finished off with a narrow band of rib.

Next row K8, turn.
Rep last 2 rows until all of the 8 sts in colour A have been knitted, ending with a P row, *do not turn.*
Still with B pick up and P8 sts along side edge of next rectangle. Rep from *** 5 [6] times more.
Break off B. ****
Work from * to **** 5 times more.
Join in A and commence top edge triangles.
1st row K2, turn.
2nd row P2, turn.
3rd row Inc in first st, sl 1, K1, psso, turn.
4th row P3, turn.
5th row Inc in first st, K1, sl 1, K1, psso, turn.
6th row P4, turn.
7th row Inc in first st, K2, sl 1, K1, psso, turn.
8th row P5, turn.
9th row K2 tog, K2, sl 1, K1, psso, turn.
10th row P4, turn.
11th row K2 tog, K1, sl 1, K1, psso, turn.
12th row P3, turn.
13th row K2 tog, sl 1, K1, psso, turn.
14th row P2 tog.
*****Next row** K1.
Cont in A, pick up and K8 sts along 2nd side of next rectangle, turn.
Next row P7, P2 tog.
Next row Sl 1, K1, psso, K5, sl 1, K first st of next rectangle, psso, turn.
Next row P7.
Next row Sl 1, K1, psso, K4, sl 1, K1 as before, psso, turn.
Next row P6.
Next row Sl 1, K1, psso, K3, sl 1, K1 as before, psso, turn.

Next row P5.
Next row Sl 1, K1, psso, K2, sl 1, K1 as before, psso, turn.
Next row P4.
Next row Sl 1, K1, psso, K1, sl 1, K1 as before, psso, turn.
Next row P3.
Next row Sl 1, K1, psso, sl 1, K1 as before, psso, turn.
Next row P2.
Next row K1, sl 1, K1 as before, psso, K1, turn.
Next row Sl 1, P2 tog, psso.
Rep from ***** 4 [5] times more.
Pick up and K8 sts down 2nd side of last rectange, turn.
1st row P7, P2 tog.
2nd row Sl 1, K1, psso, K4, K2 tog.
3rd row P6.
4th row Sl 1, K1, psso, K2, K2 tog.
5th row P4.
6th row Sl 1, K1, psso, K2 tog.
7th row P2.
8th row K2 tog and fasten off.

Neckband

With Rs facing, 3¾mm/No 9 needles and A pick up and K102 [120] sts evenly across top edge.
Work 2cm/¾in K1, P1 rib.
Cast off in rib.

Front

Work as given for back.

Sleeves

With 3¾mm/No 9 needles and A cast on 42 sts.
Work 5cm/2in K1, P1 rib, ending with a Ws row.
Next row (inc row) Rib 2, (inc in next st, rib 6) 5 times, inc in next st, rib 4. 48 sts.
Change to 4½mm/No 7 needles.
Break off A and join in B.
Both sizes Work in patt as given for first size on back to ****.
Join in A and work from * to **** 3 times more.
Work from * to *** once more.
Commence top edge triangles.
1st row K8, turn.
2nd row P2 tog, P5, P tog last st in colour B with first of next 8 sts on left-hand needle in colour A, turn.
3rd row K7, turn.
4th row P2 tog, P4, P2 tog as before, turn.
5th row K6, turn.
Cont in this way until one st rem.
Pick up and P7 sts along side of next rectangle, turn.
Rep from 1st row 5 times more.
Fasten off.
With Rs facing, 3¾mm/No 9 needles and A pick up and K102 sts evenly across top of sleeve. Work 2cm/¾in K1, P1 rib. Cast off in rib.

To make up

Join shoulder seams for 14cm/5½in. Join sleeve seams. Join side seams leaving 23cm/9in open for armholes. Sew in sleeves.

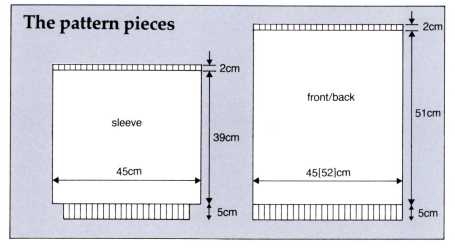

The pattern pieces

sleeve

45cm

2cm

39cm

5cm

front/back

45[52]cm

2cm

51cm

5cm

Woven cluster cardigan

The main fabric of this tweed cardigan is covered with woven clusters, worked using a cable needle. There are also panels of cables on the sleeves and front which are also decorated with woven clusters.

Sizes

To fit 86 [94]cm/34 [37]in bust loosely
Length to shoulder, 64 [66]cm/ 25¼ [26]in
Sleeve seam, 46cm/18in
The figures in [] refer to the 94 cm/ 37in size only

You will need

19 [21]×50g balls of Sunbeam Aran Tweed (100% wool)
One pair 3¾mm/No 9 needles
One pair 4½mm/No 7 needles
One cable needle
Seven buttons

Tension

20 sts and 28 rows to 10cm/4in over st st worked on 4½mm/No 7 needles

Back

With 3¾mm/No 9 needles cast on 103 [111] sts.
1st row P1, *K1, P1, rep from *to end.
2nd row K1, *P1, K1, rep from * to end.
Rep these 2 rows for 8cm/3¼in, ending with a 1st row.
Change to 4½mm/No 7 needles.
Next row (set position of patts) K6, P21 [25] sts, K4, (P4, K4) twice, P1, K7, P1, K4, (P4, K4) twice, P21 [25] sts, K6.
Commence cluster and cable patt.
1st row (Rs) P6, K21 [25] sts, P4, sl next 2 sts on to cable needle and hold at back of work, K2, K2 from cable needle – **called C4B**, P4, sl next 2 sts on to cable needle and hold at front of work, K2, K2 from cable needle – **called C4F**, P4, K1, P7, K1, P4, C4B, P4, C4F, P4, K21 [25] sts, P6.
2nd row K6, P21 [25] sts, K4, (P4, K4) twice, P1, K7, P1, K4, (P4, K4) twice, P21 [25] sts, K6.

Left: This casual, long-line cardigan is knitted in a warm tweedy yarn. It buttons up to a round neck, and the neckband is folded over to the right side and stitched neatly into place.

3rd row P6, K5 [1], (sl next 3 sts on to cable needle and hold at front of work, wind yarn across back and round front of these 3sts 6 times then back between needles, sl 3 sts back on to left-hand needle and K them – **called cl 3**, K5) 2 [3] times, P3,(sl next st on to cable needle and hold at back of work, K2, P1 from cable needle – **called cr3R**, sl next 2 sts on to cable needle and hold at front of work, P1, K2 from cable needle – **called cr3L**, P2) twice, P1, K1, P7, K1, P3,(cr3R, cr3L, P2) twice, P1, K5 [1], (cl 3, K5) 2 [3] times, P6.
4th row K6, P21 [25] sts, K3, (P2, K2) 4 times, K1, P1, K7, P1, K3, (P2, K2) 4 times, K1, P21 [25] sts, K6.
5th row P6, K21 [25] sts, P2, (cr3R, P2, cr3L) twice, P2, K1, P7, K1, P2, (cr3R, P2, cr3L) twice, P2, K21 [25] sts, P6.
6th row K6, P21 [25] sts, K2, P2, K4, P4, K4, P2, K2, P1, K7, P1, K2, P2, K4, P4, K4, P2, K2, P21 [25] sts, K6.
7th row P6, K1 [5], (cl 3, K5) twice, cl 3, K1, P2, K2, P4, C4B, P4, K2, P2, K1, P7, K1, P2, K2, P4, C4B, P4, K2, P2, K1 [5], (cl 3, K5) twice, cl 3, K1, P6.
8th row As 6th.
9th row P6, K21 [25] sts, P2, K2, P4, K4, P4, K2, P2, K1, P7, K2, P2, K2, P4, K4, P4, K2, P2, K21 [25] sts, P6.
10th row As 6th.
11th row P6, K5 [1], (cl 3, K5) 2 [3] times, P2, K2, P4, C4B, P4, K2, P2, K1, P7, K1, P2, K2, P4, C4B, P4, K2, P2, K5 [1], (cl 3, K5) 2 [3] times, P6.
12th row As 6th.
13th row P6, K21 [25] sts, P2, (cr3L, P2, cr3R) twice, P2, K1, P7, K1, P2, (cr3L, P2, cr3R) twice, P2, K21 [25] sts, P6.
14th row As 4th
15th row P6, K1 [5], (cl 3, K5) twice, cl 3, K1, P3, (cr3L, cr3R, P2) twice, P1, K1, P7, K1, P3, (cr3L, cr3R, P2) twice, P1, K1 [5], (cl 3, K5) twice, cl 3, K1, P6.
16th row As 2nd.
17th row As 1st.
18th row As 2nd.
19th row As 3rd.
20th row As 4th.
21st row P6, K21 [25] sts, P3, (K2,

P2) twice, K2, sl the last 6 sts just worked on to cable needle and hold at front of work, wind yarn across front and round to back 4 times, sl 6 sts back on to right-hand needle – **called cl 6**, P2, K2, P3, K1, P7, K1, P3, (K2, P2) twice, K2, cl 6, P2, K2, P3, K21 [25] sts, P6.
22nd row As 4th.
23rd row As 15th.
24th row As 2nd.
These 24 rows form patt and are rep throughout.
Cont in patt until work measures 42cm/16½in from beg, ending with a Ws row.

Shape armholes
Cast off 6 sts at beg of next 2 rows. 91 [99] sts.
Cont without shaping until armholes measure 22 [24] cm/ 8¾ [9½]in from beg, ending with a Ws row.

Shape shoulders
Cast off at beg of next and every row 6 sts 4 times and 5 [7] sts 4 times. Leave rem 47 sts on holder for centre back neck.

Left front
With 3¾mm/No 9 needles cast on 49 [53] sts. Work 8cm/3¼in rib as given for back, ending with a 1st row.
Change to 4½mm/No 7 needles.**
Next row (set position of patts) K1, P1, K4, (P4, K4) twice, P21 [25] sts, K6.
Commence cluster and cable patt.
1st row (Rs) P6, K21 [25] sts, P4, C4B, P4, C4F, P4, K1, P1.
2nd row K1, P1, K4, (P4, K4) twice, P21 [25] sts, K6.
Cont in patt as now set until work measures same as back to underarm, ending with the same patt row.

Shape armhole
Cast off 6 sts at beg of next row. 43 [47] sts.
Cont without shaping until armhole measures 16 [18]cm/6¼ [7]in from beg, ending with a Rs row.

Shape neck
Cast off at beg of next and every alt row 9 sts once, 3 sts once, 2 sts 3 times, then dec one st at same edge on foll 3 alt rows. 22 [26] sts.
Cont if necessary without shaping until armhole measures same as back to shoulder, ending at armhole edge.

Shape shoulder
Cast off at beg of next and every alt row 6 sts twice and 5 [7] sts twice.

Right front
Work as given for left front to**.
Next row (set position of patts) K6, P21 [25] sts, K4, (P4, K4) twice, P1, K1.
Commence cluster and cable patt.
1st row (Rs) P1, K1, P4, C4B, P4, C4F, P4, K21 [25] sts, P6.
Cont in patt as now set and complete to match left front, reversing all shapings.

Sleeves
With 3¾mm/No 9 needles cast on 41 [45] sts. Work 5cm/2in rib as given for back, ending with a 1st row and inc 5 [9] sts evenly in last row. 46 [54] sts.
Change to 4½mm/No 7 needles.
Next row (set position of patts) P13 [17] sts, K4, (P4, K4) twice, P13 [17] sts.
Commence cluster and cable patt.
1st row (Rs) K13 [17] sts, P4, C4B, P4, C4F, P4, K to end.
2nd row P13 [17] sts, K4, (P4, K4) twice, P to end.
3rd row K5 [1], (cl 3, K5) 1 [2] times, P3, (cr3R, cr3L, P2) twice, P1, (K5, cl 3) 1 [2] times, K5 [1].
Cont in patt as now set, inc one st at each end of 7th and every foll 6th row, working the extra sts into cluster patt, until there are 21 [25] sts in each cluster panel, then work inc sts into reverse st st until there are 86 [94] sts.
Cont without shaping until sleeve measures 49cm/19¼in, or 3cm/1¼in more than required length to underarm, ending with a Ws row.
Cast off very loosely.

Right front band
With 3¾mm/No 9 needles and Rs of work facing, pick up and K124 [130] sts evenly up right front edge.
Next row *K1, P1, rep from * to end.
Work 2 more rows in rib as now set.
Next row (buttonhole row) Rib 7 sts, (cast off 3 sts, rib 17 [18] sts) 5 times, cast off 3 sts, rib 14 [15] sts.
Next row Rib to end, casting on 3 sts above those cast off in previous row.
Work 3 more rows in rib. Cast off in rib.

Left front band
Work to match right front band, noting that 1st row will read *P1, K1, rep from * to end, and omitting buttonholes.

Neckband
Join shoulder seams. With 3¾mm/ No 9 needles and Rs of work facing, pick up and K33 sts up right front neck, K across back neck sts and pick up and K33 sts down left front neck. 113 [113] sts.
Next row P1, *K1, P1, rep from * to end.
Work 2 more rows in rib as now set.
Next row (buttonhole row) Rib 3 sts, cast off 3 sts, rib to end.
Next row Rib to end, casting on 3 sts above those cast off in previous row.
Cont in rib for 5cm/2in, then rep the 2 buttonhole rows. Work a further 4 rows in rib. Cast off very loosely.

To make up
Do not press as this will flatten the patt. Set in sleeves, sewing last 3cm/1¼in to cast off sts at underarm on body. Join side and sleeve seams. Fold neckband in half to outside and sl st in place, sewing round double buttonhole. Sew on buttons.

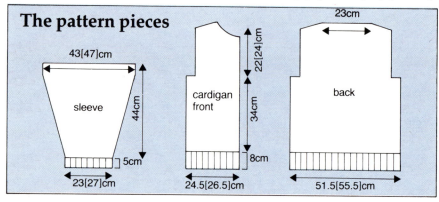

The pattern pieces

43[47]cm
sleeve
44cm
5cm
23[27]cm

cardigan front
34cm
8cm
22[24]cm
24.5[26.5]cm

23cm
back
51.5[55.5]cm

Cable jacket

Multi-twisted cables decorate the body and sleeves of this beautiful jacket. The cable pattern needs concentration but as it is repeated it gets easier as you go along.

All the borders are worked in Irish moss stitch and the top of the sleeves include dart shaping in moss stitch. Shoulder pads can be inserted if you wish.

Sizes

To fit 86 [91:97]cm/34 [36:38]in bust
Length to shoulder, 55 [57:59]cm/21¾ [22½:23¼]in
Sleeve seam, 40cm/15¾in
The figures in [] refer to the 91/36 and 97cm/38in sizes respectively

You will need

10 [11:12] × 50g balls of Lister-Lee Thermoknit for Aran (50% polypropylene, 30% acrylic, 20% wool)
One pair 4½mm/No 7 needles
One pair 5mm/No 6 needles
One cable needle
Five buttons

Left: Beautiful, intricate cables are the main feature on this jacket. Wear it belted or thread a twisted cord through the eyelet holes at the waist.

Tension

18 sts and 22 rows to 10cm/4in over st st worked on 5mm/No 6 needles

Cable pattern panel

This panel is worked over 20 sts, which inc to 30 sts as the pattern is worked.
1st row P10, pick up loop lying between needles and K tbl – **called M1K**, P10.
2nd row K10, M1K, P twice into next st, M1K, K10.
3rd row P9, (sl next st on to cable needle and hold at back of work, K next 2 sts tbl – **called K2B**, P1 from cable needle – **called cr3R**), (sl next 2 sts on to cable needle and hold at front of work, P1, K2B from cable needle – **called cr3L**), P9.
4th row K8, (sl next st on to cable needle and hold at front of work, P next 2 sts tbl – **called P2B**, K1 from cable needle – **called tw3R**), K2, (sl next 2 sts on to cable needle and hold at back of work, K1, P2B from cable needle – **called tw3L**), K8.
5th row P8, K2B, P4, K2B, P8.
6th row K8, P2B, K4, P2B, K8.
7th row P8, (sl next 2 sts on to cable needle and hold at front of work, K1, K2B from cable needle – **called cr3LK**), P2, (sl next st on to cable needle and hold at back of work, K2B, K1 from cable needle – **called cr3RK**), P8.
8th row K8, P next st tbl – **called P1B**, M1K, tw3L, tw3R, M1K, P1B, K8.
9th row P7, cr3R, P1, (sl next 2 sts on to cable needle and hold at back of work, K2B, K2B from cable needle – **called cr4K**), P1, cr3L, P7.
10th row K6, tw3R, K2, P next 4 sts tbl – **called P4B**, K2, tw3L, K6.
11th row P5, cr3R, P3, K next 4 sts tbl – **called K4B**, P3, cr3L, P5.
12th row K5, P2B, K4, P4B, K4, P2B, K5.
13th row P5, K2B, P4, K4B, P4, K2B, P5.
14th row K5, (sl next 2 sts on to cable needle and hold at back of work, P1, P2B from cable needle – **called tw3LP**), K3, (sl next 2 sts on to cable needle and hold at back of work, P2B, P2B from cable needle – **called cr4P**), K3, (sl next st on to cable needle and hold at front of work, P2B, P1 from cable needle – **called tw3RP**), K5.
15th row P5, K next st tbl – **called K1B**, M1K, cr3L, P2, K4B, P2, cr3R, M1K, K1B, P5.
16th row K4, tw3R, K1, tw3L, K1, P4B, K1, tw3R, K1, tw3L, K4.
17th row P3, cr3R, P3, cr3L, cr4K, cr3R, P3, cr3L, P3.
18th row K3, P2B, K5, tw3L, P2B, tw3R, K5, P2B, K3.
19th row P3, K2B, pick up loop lying between sts and P tbl – **called M1P**, P6, cr3L, cr3R, P6, M1P, K2B, P3. 30 sts.

Cable abbreviations used in this pattern

Note: Throughout these abbreviations, the front of work means the side which is facing you and the back of work means side away from you, regardless of Rs or Ws pattern row. Cable needle is referred to as cn.

K1B	K next 1, 2 or 4 sts
K2B	through back of loop
K4B	
P1B	P next 1, 2 or 4 sts
P2B	through back of loop
P4B	
M1K	pick up loop between sts and K tbl
M1P	pick up loop between sts and P tbl
cr3R	sl next st on to cable needle (cn) and hold at back of work, K2B, P1 from cn
tw3L	sl next 2 sts on to cn and hold at back of work, K1, P2B from cn
cr3L	sl next 2 sts on to cn and hold at front of work, P1, K2B from cn
tw3R	sl next st on to cn and hold at front of work, P2B, K1 from cn
cr3RK	sl next st on to cn and hold at back of work, K2B, K1 from cn
tw3LP	sl next 2 sts on to cn and hold at back of work, P1, P2B from cn
cr3LK	sl next 2 sts on to cn and hold at front of work, K1, K2B from cn
tw3RP	sl next st on to cn and hold at front of work, P2B, P1 from cn
cr4K	sl next 2 sts on to cn and hold at back of work, K2B, K2B from cn
cr4P	sl next 2 sts on to cn and hold at back of work, P2B, P2B from cn
tw2RP	sl next st on to cn and hold at front of work, P1B, P1B from cn
tw2LP	sl next st on to cn and hold at back of work, P1B, P1B from cn
cr2R	sl next st on to cn and hold at back of work, K1B, P1 from cn
tw2L	sl next st on to cn and hold at back of work, K1, P1B from cn
cr2L	sl next st on to cn and hold at front of work, P1, K1B from cn
tw2R	sl next st on to cn and hold at front of work, P1B, K1 from cn

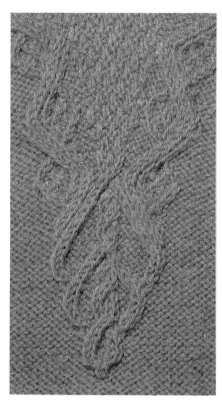

Above: An alternative colourway showing a detail of the moss stitch dart incorporated in the cable panel.

20th row K3, tw3L, K7, cr4P, K7, tw3R, K3.

21st row P3, K1B, cr3L, P6, K4B, P6, cr3R, K1B, P3.

22nd row K3, (sl next st on to cable needle and hold at back of work, P1B, P1B from cable needle – **called tw2LP**), tw3L, K5, P4B, K5, tw3R, (sl next st on cable needle and hold at front of work, P1B, P1B from cable needle – **called tw2RP**), K3.

23rd row P3, (cr3L) twice, P4, K4B, P4, (cr3R) twice, P3.

24th row K4, (tw3L) twice, K3, cr4P, K3, (tw3R) twice, K4.

25th row P5, (cr3L) twice, P2, K4B, P2, (cr3R) twice, P5.

26th row K4, tw2RP, (tw3L) twice, K1, P4B, K1, (tw3R) twice, tw2LP, K4.

27th row P3, (sl next st on to cable needle and hold at back of work, K1B, P1 from cable needle – **called cr2R**), (sl next st on to cable needle and hold at front of work, P1, K1B from cable needle – **called cr2L**), (cr3L) twice, cr4K, (cr3R) twice, cr2R, cr2L, P3.

28th row K2, tw2RP, K2, tw2LP, (tw3L) twice, P2B, (tw3R) twice, tw2RP, K2, tw2LP, K2.

29th row P1, (cr2R, cr2L) twice, (cr3L) twice, (cr3R) twice, (cr2R, cr2L) twice, P1.

30th row K1, P1B, K2, tw2RP, K2, P1B, K1, P2B, K1, cr4P, K1, P2B, K1, P1B, K2, tw2LP, K2, P1B, K1.

31st row P1, (cr2L, cr2R) twice, cr3R, P1, K4B, P1, cr3L, (cr2L, cr2R) twice, P1.

32nd row K2, (sl next st on to cable needle and hold at back of work, K1, P1B from cable needle – **called tw2L**), K2, (sl next st on to cable needle and hold at front of work, P1B, K1 from cable needle – **called tw2R**), tw3R, K2, P4B, K2, tw3L, tw2L, K2, tw2R, K2.

33rd row P3, cr2L, cr2R, cr3R, P3, K4B, P3, cr3L, cr2L, cr2R, P3.

34th row K4, tw2R, tw3R, K4, P4B, K4, tw3L, tw2L, K4.

35th row P3, cr2R, cr3R, P5, cr4K, P5, cr3L, cr2L, P3.

36th row K2, tw2R, tw3R, tw2LP, K4, P4B, K4, tw2RP, tw3L, tw2L, K2.

37th row P1, cr2R, cr3R, cr2R, cr2L, P3, K4B, P3, cr2R, cr2L, cr3L, cr2L, P1.

38th row Tw2R, tw3R, tw2RP, K2, tw2LP, K2, P4B, K2, tw2RP, K2, tw2LP, tw3L, tw2L.

39th row P1, cr3R, (cr2R, cr2L) twice, P1, K4B, P1, (cr2R, cr2L) twice, cr3L, P1.

40th row K1, P2B, K1, P1B, K2, tw2LP, K2, P1B, K1, cr4P, K1, P1B, K2, tw2RP, K2, P1B, K1, P2B, K1.

41st row P1, cr3L, (cr2L, cr2R) twice, P1, K4B, P1, (cr2L, cr2R) twice, cr3R, P1.

42nd row K2, tw3L, tw2L, K2, tw2R, K2, P4B, K2, tw2L, K2, tw2R, tw3R, K2.

43rd row P3, cr3L, cr2L, cr2R, P3, K4B, P3, cr2L, cr2R, cr3R, P3.

44th row K4, tw3L, tw2L, K4, P4B, K4, tw2R, tw3R, K4.

45th row P5, cr3L, cr2L, P3, cr4K, P3, cr2R, cr3R, P5.

46th row K4, tw2RP, tw3L, tw2L, K2, P4B, K2, tw2R, tw3R, tw2LP, K4.

47th row P3, cr2R, cr2L, cr3L, cr2L, P1, K4B, P1, cr2R, cr3R, cr2R, cr2L, P3.

48th row K2, tw2RP, K2, tw2LP, tw3L, tw2L, P4B, tw2R, tw3R, tw2RP, K2, tw2LP, K2.

49th row P1, (cr2R, cr2L) twice, cr3L, P1, K4B, P1, cr3R, (cr2R, cr2L) twice, P1.

Rep from 30th to 49th rows inclusive throughout.

Back

With 4½mm/No 7 needles cast on 83 [87:91] sts. Commence Irish moss st.

1st row (Rs) K1, *P1, K1, rep from * to end.

2nd row P1, *K1, P1, rep from * to end.

3rd row as 2nd.

4th row as 1st.

Rep these 4 rows for 10cm/4in, ending with a Ws row and inc one st at end of last row. 84 [88:92] sts. Change to 5mm/No 6 needles.

Next row (eyelet hole row) K3, *yfwd, K2 tog, K2, rep from * to last st, K1.

Beg with a K row cont in reversed st st until work measures 23 [24:25]cm/ 9 [9½:9¾]in from beg, ending with a K row.

Commence cable patt, or cont in reversed st st, noting that sts will not be increased in this event.

Next row P10 [11:12] sts, work 1st row of cable panel, P24 [26:28] sts, work 1st row of cable panel, P10 [11:12] sts.

Next row K10 [11:12] sts, work 2nd row of cable panel, K24 [26:28] sts, work 2nd row of cable panel, K10 [11:12] sts.

Keeping each end and centre in reversed st st and beg with 3rd row on cable panel, cont in patt as now set, noting that after 19th row of panel there will be 104 [108:112] sts. Cont until work measures 35 [36:37]cm/13¾ [14¼:14½]in from beg, ending with a Ws row.

Shape armholes

Keeping patt correct throughout, cast off at beg of next and every row 3 sts twice and 2 sts twice. Dec one st at each end of next and foll 3 [4:5] alt rows. 86 [88:90] sts. Cont without shaping until armholes measure 18 [19:20]cm/ 7 [7½:7¾]in from beg, ending with a Ws row.

Shape neck

Next row Patt 35 sts, turn and leave rem sts on holder.

Complete right shoulder first.

Cast off 2 sts at beg of next row for neck. Dec one st at beg of foll alt row for neck, ending with a Ws row.

Shape shoulder

Cast off rem 32 sts for shoulder.

With Rs of work facing, rejoin yarn to rem sts on holder, cast off first 16 [18:20] sts loosely, patt to end. Work 1 row. Complete to match right shoulder, reversing shaping.

Left front

With 4½mm/No 7 needles cast on 45 [47:51] sts. Work 10cm/4in moss st as given for back, ending with a Ws row and inc 1 [2:1] sts in last row. 46 [49:52] sts.
Change to 5mm/No 6 needles.**
Next row (eyelet hole row) *K2, K2 tog, yfwd, rep from * to last 6 [9:8] sts, K0 [3:2] sts, moss st 6 sts.
Next row Moss st 6 sts, K to end.
Keeping 6 sts at front edge in moss st throughout, cont in reversed st st until work measures 23 [24:25]cm/9 [9½:9¾]in from beg, ending with a K row.
Commence cable patt.
Next row P10 [11:12] sts, work 1st row of cable panel, P10 [12:14] sts, moss st 6.
Next row Moss st 6 sts, K10 [12:14] sts, work 2nd row of cable panel, K10 [11:12] sts.
Keeping moss st and reversed st st correct, beg with 3rd row of cable panel and cont in patt as now set noting that after 19th row of panel there will be 56 [59:62] sts.
Cont until work measures same as back to underarm, ending with a Ws row.

Shape armhole

Keeping patt correct throughout, cast off at beg of next and foll alt row 3 sts once and 2 sts once. Dec one st at beg of foll 4 [5:6] alt rows. 47 [49:51] sts.
Cont without shaping until armhole measures 10 [11:12]cm/4 [4¼:4¾]in from beg, ending with a Ws row.

Shape neck

Next row Patt to last 6 sts, turn and leave these 6 sts on safety pin.
Cast off at beg of next and every alt row 2 sts 2 [3:4] times. Dec one st at beg of foll 5 alt rows. 32 sts.
Cont without shaping until armhole measures same as back to shoulder, ending with a Ws row.
Cast off.
Mark positions of 5 buttons on front band, first to come 15cm/6in from beg and last to come on last Rs row before neck shaping, with 3 more evenly spaced between.

Right front

Work to match left front to **
Next row (eyelet hole row) Moss st 6 sts, K0 [3:2] sts, *yfwd, K2 tog, K2, rep from * to end.
Cont as given for left front reversing position of cable panel, all shapings and making buttonholes as markers are reached on Rs rows as foll:
Next row (buttonhole row) Moss st 3 sts, cast off one st, patt to end.
Next row Patt to end, casting on one st above st cast off in previous row.

Sleeves

With 4½mm/No 7 needles cast on 43 [45:47] sts. Work 3cm/1¼in moss st as given for back, ending with a Ws row and inc one st at end of last row. 44 [46:48] sts.
Change to 5mm/No 6 needles. K one row.
Beg with a K row cont in reversed st st, inc one st at each end of every 8th row 10 times in all, *at the same time* when work measures 31cm/12¼in from beg, ending with a K row, work first 20 rows of cable panel in centre of sleeve sts. 74 [76:78] sts.

Shape top

Keeping patt correct throughout, cast off at beg of next and every row 3 sts 4 times, 2 sts 4 times and one st twice. 52 [54:56] sts.

Shape dart

Next row (31st cable panel row) Patt 24 [25:26] sts, (K1, P1, M1K, P1, K1, for dart), patt 24 [25:26] sts.

Next row Patt to centre 5 sts, P1, (K1, P1) twice, patt to end.
Next row P2 tog, patt to centre 5 sts, P1, (K1, P1) twice, patt to last 2 sts, P2 tog.
Next row Patt to centre 5 sts, K1, (P1, K1) twice, patt to end.
Next row Patt to centre 5 sts, M1P, K1, (P1, K1) twice, M1P, patt to end.
Next row Patt to centre 7 sts, moss st 7 as now set, patt to end.
Keeping centre dart sts in moss st as now set, inc one st on each side of these sts on 41st, 45th, 51st and 55th rows of patt, *at the same time* dec one st at each end of next and every foll 4th row 4 times in all, then at each end of foll 3 alt rows, ending with a Ws row. 47 [49:51] sts.
Cast off at beg of next and every row 2 sts twice and 43 [45:47] sts once.

Neckband

Join shoulder seams. With Rs of work facing and 4½mm/No 7 needles moss st across 6 sts of right front, pick up and K63 [65:67] sts round neck, then moss st across 6 sts of left front.
Work 3cm/1¼in moss st. Cast off in patt.

To make up

Do not press. Sew in sleeves easing in top to fit armholes. Join side and sleeve seams. Sew on buttons. Using 2 strands of yarn make a twisted cord about 100cm/40in long and thread through eyelet holes at waist.

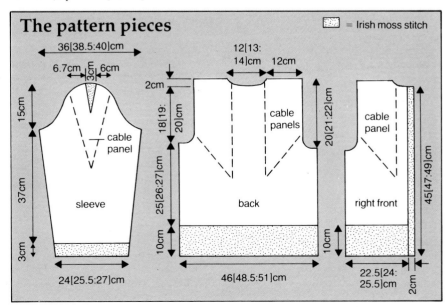

The pattern pieces   = Irish moss stitch

36[38.5:40]cm
6.7cm · 3cm · 6cm
2cm
15cm
cable panel
37cm
sleeve
3cm
24[25.5:27]cm

12[13:14]cm 12cm
18[19:20]cm
cable panels
25[26:27]cm
back
10cm
46[48.5:51]cm

20[21:22]cm
cable panel
right front
10cm
22.5[24:25.5]cm
2cm
45[47:49]cm

Stitch sampler jersey

This jersey is worked in a variety of stitches and colours to give a sampler effect. The simple style has the minimum of shaping, with a garter stitch welt and cuffs and a plain ribbed neckband.

Sizes

To fit 81 [86:91]cm/32 [34:36]in bust
Length to shoulder, 68 [69:70]cm/ 26¾ [27¼:27½]in
Sleeve seam, 51cm/20in
The figures in [] refer to the 86cm/ 34in and 91cm/36in sizes respectively

You will need

6 [6:7]×50g balls of 3 Suisses Suizasport (55% acrylic, 45% wool) in main colour A
6 [6:7] balls of same in contrast colour B
3 balls each of same in contrast colours C and D
1 [1:2] balls of same in contrast colour E
One pair 5mm/No 6 needles
One pair 6mm/No 4 needles
Set of four 5mm/No 6 needles pointed at both ends

Tension

15 sts and 22 rows to 10cm/4in over st st worked on 6mm/No 4 needles
15 sts and about 20 rows to 10cm/4in over patt worked on 6mm/No 4 needles, noting that tension varies slightly over different stitch patts

Back

With 5mm/No 6 needles and A cast on 54 [58:62] sts and work 7 rows in g st.

Next row (inc row) K5 [2:4], *inc 1 by picking up loop lying between sts and K into back of it –**called M1**, K4 [5:5], rep from * to last 5 [1:3] sts, M1, K5 [1:3]. 66 [70:74] sts.
Change to 6mm/No 4 needles. Commence patt.
1st row (Rs) K2 A, *K2 D, K2 A, rep from * to end.
2nd row P2 A, *P2 D, P2 A, rep from * to end.
3rd row K2 D, *K2 A, K2 D, rep from * to end.
4th row P2 D, *P2 A, P2 D, rep from * to end.
5th to 8th rows As 1st to 4th.
9th to 12th rows Change to 5mm/ No 6 needles and using D, work 4 rows in g st, inc one st at end of last row. 67 [71:75] sts.
Change to 6mm/No 4 needles and B.
13th row P1 [3:5], *K5, P5, rep from * to last 6 [8:10] sts, K5, P1 [3:5].
14th row K1 [3:5], *P5, K5, rep from * to last 6 [8:10] sts, P5, K1 [3:5].
15th and 16th rows As 13th and 14th.
17th row As 14th.
18th row As 13th.
19th and 20th rows As 17th and 18th.
21st to 24th rows As 13th to 16th.
25th to 28th rows With C, beg with a K row work 4 rows st st.
29th row K3 C, *K1 B, K3 C, rep from * to end.
30th row P3 C, *P1 B, P3 C, rep from * to end.
31st row With C, K to end.
32nd row With C, P to end.
33rd row K1 B, *K1 C, K1 B, rep from * to end.
34th row P1 C, *P1 B, P1 C, rep from * to end.
35th and 36th rows As 33rd and 34th.

37th to 40th rows Change to 5mm/ No 6 needles and using B, work 4 rows in g st, dec 1 st at beg of first row. 66 [70:74] sts.
Change to 6mm/No 4 needles and A.
41st row P3 [5:1], *K4, (K1, P1) twice, P4, rep from * to last 3 [5:1] sts, K to end.
42nd row P3 [5:1], *K4, (P1, K1) twice, P4, rep from * to last 3 [5:1] sts, K to end.
43rd and 44th rows As 41st and 42nd.
45th row P1, (K1, P1) 1 [2:0] times, *P4, K4, (K1, P1) twice, rep from * to last 3 [5:1] sts, P to end.
46th row K3 [5:1], *(P1, K1) twice, P4, K4, rep from * to last 3 [5:1] sts, (P1, K1) 1 [2:0] times, P1.
47th and 48th row As 45th and 46th.
49th row K3 [5:1], *(K1, P1) twice, P4, K4, rep from * to last 3 [5:1] sts, (K1, P1) 1 [2:0] times, K1.
50th row K1, (P1, K1) 1 [2:0] times, *P4, K4, (P1, K1) twice, rep from * to last 3 [5:1] sts, P to end.
51st and 52nd rows As 49th and 50th.
53rd to 58th rows With E, work 6 rows in moss st, inc one st at end of last row. 67 [71:75] sts.
59th and 60th rows With B, beg with a K row work 2 rows in st st.
61st row K3 [5:1], *P1, K5, rep from * to last 4 [6:2] sts, P1, K3 [5:1].
62nd and 63rd rows Beg with a P row work 2 rows in st st.
64th row P0 [2:4], *K1, P5, rep from * to last 1 [3:5] sts, K1, P0 [2:4].
65th to 68th rows As 59th to 62nd, dec one st at end of last row. 66 [70:74] sts.
69th to 90th rows Change to 5mm/ No 6 needles. Cont in g st working 2 rows in each of D, B, C, B, E, B, D, B, A, B and E.
91st to 98th rows Change to 6mm/ No 4 needles and A. Beg with K row work 8 rows in st st.
These 98 rows form the patt. Cont in patt until back measures 68 [69:70]cm/26¾ [27¼:27½]in from beg, or length required, ending with a Ws row, and noting that number of sts at end of last row will be 66 [70:74].

Shape shoulders

Keeping patt correct, cast off at beg of every row 7 [7:8] sts twice, 7 [8:8] sts twice and 7 sts twice.
Leave rem 24 [26:28] sts on a holder.

Front

Work as given for back until 12 rows

The pattern pieces

sleeve
51cm
40[43:45]cm
28cm
23cm

front
16[17:18]cm
68[69:70]cm
45[47:50]cm
36[39:41]cm

back
16[17:18]cm
45[47:50]cm
36[39:41]cm

less than back to shoulders, ending with a Ws row, noting that number of sts at end of last row will be 67 [71:75].

Shape neck

Next row Keeping patt correct work across 29 [30:31] sts, turn and leave rem sts on a holder.
Complete left shoulder first.
Cast off 2 sts at beg of next and foll alt row, then dec one st at beg of foll 4 alt rows, ending with a Ws row.

Shape shoulder

Cast off at beg of next and every foll alt row 7 [7:8] sts once, 7 [8:8] sts once and 7 sts once.
With Rs of work facing sl the first 9 [11:13] sts from holder on to a 2nd holder for front neck.
Rejoin yarn to rem sts for right shoulder and patt to end.
Work one row in patt, then complete to match left shoulder, reversing all shaping.

Sleeves

With 5mm/No 6 needles and A cast on 34 sts. Work 7 rows in g st.
Next row (inc row) K3, (M1, K4) 7 times, M1, K3. 42 sts.
Change to 6mm/No 4 needles.
Taking care to work extra sts into patt, work in patt as given for back, inc one st each end of the 9th and every foll 10th [8th:7th] row until there are 60 [64:68] sts.
Cont in patt without shaping until 96 rows have been worked from beg of patt. Cast off loosely.

Neckband

Join shoulder seams. With Rs facing, set of four 5mm/No 6 needles and A, K across 24 [26:28] sts on holder for back neck dec 3 sts evenly across them, pick up and K14 sts down left front neck, K across 9 [11:13] sts on holder from front neck dec 2 sts evenly across them, pick up and K14 sts up right front neck. 56 [60:64] sts.
Work 6 rounds K1, P1 rib.
Cast off loosely in rib.

To make up

Do not press. Sew in sleeves.
Join side and sleeve seams.

Right: Check you have the right number of stitches before starting any shaping on this multi-patterned jersey.

Two-colour mohair jersey

Knit this geometric style jersey in dramatically contrasting colours to complete a striking outfit for day or evening wear.

It has three-quarter length batwing sleeves and a ribbed welt which fits snugly around the waist. It is not difficult to knit as the main pattern pieces are entirely in stocking stitch and the diagonal is formed by changing colour on each row. Take care when doing this (see note opposite), otherwise a row of holes will appear on the finished garment. The colours are reversed on the back, so that each sleeve is knitted in a single colour.

Sizes

To fit 86–91cm/34–36in bust loosely
Length to centre back neck, 54.5cm/21½in
Sleeve seam, 44.5cm/17½in

You will need

4×50g balls of Pingouin Mohair 70 (70% mohair, 30% acrylic) in main colour A
3 balls of same in contrast colour B
One pair 3¼mm/No 10 needles
One pair 2¾mm/No 12 needles

Tension

22 sts and 32 rows to 10cm/4in over st st worked on 3¼mm/No 10 needles

Note

Always twist yarns round each other at back of work when changing colour

Front

With 2¾mm/No 12 needles and A cast on 103 sts.
1st row (Rs) K1, *P1, K1, rep from * to end.
2nd row P1, *K1, P1, rep from * to end.
Rep these 2 rows 12 times more, inc one st at end of last row. 104 sts.
Beg with a K row work 2 rows st st. Join in B. Cont in st st.**
1st row (Rs) K1 B, 103 A.
2nd row P102 A, 2 B.
3rd row K3 B, 101 A.
4th row P100 A, 4 B.
5th row K5 B, 99 A.
6th row P all sts in A with A and all sts in B with B.
7th row K all sts in B with B and all sts in A with A.
8th row P98 A, 6 B.
9th row K7 B, 97 A.
10th row P96 A, 8 B.
11th row K9 B, 95 A.
12th row P94 A, 10 B.
13th row K all sts in B with B and all sts in A with A.
14th row P all sts in A with A and all sts in B with B.
Cont in this way moving one st in B to the left on K rows and one st in A on P rows, then work 2 rows in colours as set, thus moving 5 sts in every 7 rows, until row

reading P20 A, 84 B has been completed.

Shape neck

Next row Keeping patt correct, K46, K12 sts and leave on holder for centre front neck, K to end. Complete right shoulder first. P one row.
Keeping patt correct throughout, dec one st at neck edge on every row until 28 sts rem.
Cont in patt without shaping until all sts in A have been worked off, ending with a K row.

Shape shoulder

Cast off at beg of next and every alt row 9 sts twice and 10 sts once.
With Ws of work shaping rejoin yarn to rem sts and complete to match first side, reversing shapings.

Back

Work as given for front to **.
1st row (Rs) K103 A, 1 B.
2nd row P2 B, 102 A.
3rd row K101 A, 3 B.
4th row P4 B, 100 A.
Working patt in opposite direction as now set, work as given for front until back measures same to shoulders, ending with a P row.

Shape shoulders

Cast off at beg of next and every row 9 sts 4 times and 10 sts twice. Leave rem 48 sts on holder for centre back neck.

Right sleeve

Mark side edges of back and front 7.5cm/3in above top of rib. With Rs of work facing, 3¼mm/No 10 needles and A, pick up and K160 sts from back marker to front marker.
Beg with a P row cont in st st, dec one st at each end of every foll 3rd row until 110 sts rem, every alt row until 78 sts rem then every row until 46 sts rem, ending with a P row.
Work 4 rows without shaping. Change to 2¾mm/No 12 needles. Work 5cm/2in K1, P1 rib. Cast off in rib.

Left sleeve

Work as given for right sleeve using B.

Neckband

Join right shoulder seam. With Rs of work facing, 2¾mm/No 12 needles and A, pick up and K42 sts down left front neck, K across front neck sts on holder, pick up and K42 sts up right front neck and K across back neck sts on holder. 144 sts.
Work 7 rows K1, P1 rib. Cast off in rib.

To make up

Do not press. Join left shoulder and neckband seam. Join side and sleeve seams.
Fold the neckband over to the wrong side and slipstitch neatly into place.

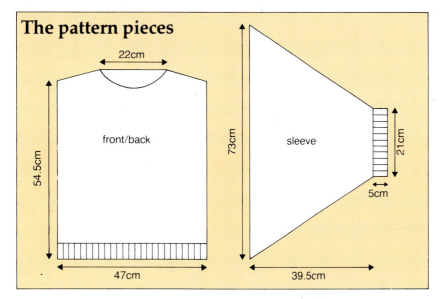

The pattern pieces

22cm
front/back
54.5cm
47cm
73cm
sleeve
21cm
5cm
39.5cm

Embroidered striped jersey

Knit this striped jersey in bold bright colours or in soft muted tones. The Swiss darning is worked in the same colour as the welt and cuffs.

Sizes

To fit 86 [91:97]cm/34 [36:38]in bust
Length to shoulder, 64 [65:66]cm/
25¼ [25½:26]in
Sleeve seam, 44cm/17¼in
The figures in [] refer to the 91/36 and the 97cm/38in sizes respectively

You will need

7 [8:8]×50g balls Argyll Ferndale Double Knitting (85% Courtelle, 15% pure wool) in main colour A
1 [2:2] balls of same in contrast colour B
1 ball of same in contrast colour C
One pair 3¼mm/No 10 needles
One pair 4mm/No 8 needles

Tension

22 sts and 30 rows to 10cm/4in over st st worked on 4mm/No 8 needles

Back

With 3¼mm/No 10 needles and C cast on 96 [102:108] sts.
Work in K1, P1 rib for 8cm/3¼in, ending with a Rs row.
Next row (inc row) Rib 6 [9:8] sts, (M1, rib 12 [12:13]) 7 times, M1, rib 6 [9:9]. 104 [110:116] sts.
Change to 4mm/No 8 needles.
Beg with a K row, work in st st and patt as follows, twisting yarn where colours join to avoid a hole.
1st row (Rs) K9 [12:15] B, K95 [98:101] A.
2nd row P95 [98:101] B, P9 [12:15] B.
3rd row In A, K to end.
4th row In A, P to end.
5th row K11 [14:17] B, K93 [96:99] A.
6th row P93 [96:99] A, P11 [14:17] B.
7th row In A, K to end.
8th row In A, P to end.
9th row K13 [16:19] B, K91 [94:97] A.
10th row P91 [94:97] A, P13 [16:19] B.
11th row In A, K to end.
12th row In A, P to end.
Cont in patt, working 2 sts more in contrast B on next and every foll 4th row until back measures 43cm/17in from beg, ending with a Ws row.

Left: The single colour and two-colour stripes form a diagonal pattern.

Shape armholes

Keeping patt correct, cast off 3 sts at beg of next 2 rows.
Dec one st at each end of next and every foll alt row until 80 [82:86] sts rem.
Cont without shaping until armholes measure 21 [22:23]cm/8¼ [8¾:9]in, ending with a Ws row.

Shape shoulders

Cast off at beg of every row 8 sts 4 times and 8 [8:9] sts twice.
Leave rem 32 [34:36] sts on holder for back neck.

Front

Work as given for back until 18 rows less than on back to shoulders, ending with a Ws row.

Shape neck

Next row (Rs) Keeping patt correct, work across 32 [33:35] sts, turn and leave rem sts on holder.
Complete left shoulder first.
Dec one st at neck edge on every row until 24 [24:25] sts rem.
Cont without shaping until front measures same as back to shoulder, ending at armhole edge.

Shape shoulder

Cast off at beg of next and every foll alt row 8 sts twice and 8 [8:9] sts once.
With Rs facing, leave the first 16 of the rem sts on holder for front neck, rejoin yarn to rem 32 [33:35] sts and complete right shoulder to match left, reversing all shaping.

Sleeves

With 3¼mm/No 10 needles and C cast on 42 [46:48] sts.
Work in K1, P1 rib for 8cm/3¼in, ending with a Rs row.
Next row (inc row) Rib 3 [5:6] sts, (M1, rib 4) 9 times, M1, rib 3[5:6]. 52 [56:58] sts.
Change to 4mm/No 8 needles and A. Beg with a K row work in st st inc one st each end of 5th and every foll 4th row until there are 94 [96:98] sts.
Cont without shaping until sleeve measures 44cm/17¼in from beg, ending with a Ws row.

Shape top

Cast off 3 sts at beg of next 2 rows.
Dec one st at each end of next and every foll alt row until 26 [26:28] sts rem, ending with a Ws row.
Cast off.

Neckband

Join right shoulder seam.
With Rs facing, 3¼mm/No 10 needles and A, pick up and K20 [22:24] sts down left side of neck, K across 16 sts on holder at centre front neck, pick up and K20 [22:24] sts up right side of neck, K across 32 [34:36] sts from back neck holder. 88 [94:100] sts.
Work in K1, P1 rib for 6cm/2¼in.
Cast off in rib.

To make up

Join left shoulder and neckband seam. Fold neckband in half and slip st into place. Join side and sleeve seams. Sew in sleeves gathering sleeve head to fit. With C, Swiss darn over 6 sts horizontally at random on the stripes worked in B as shown.

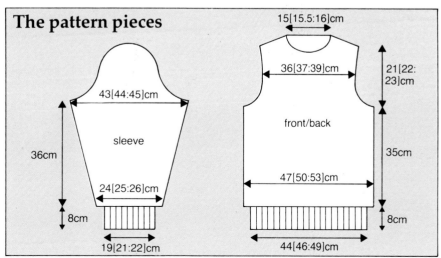

The pattern pieces

15[15.5:16]cm
36[37:39]cm
21[22:23]cm
front/back
35cm
47[50:53]cm
8cm
44[46:49]cm

43[44:45]cm
sleeve
36cm
24[25:26]cm
8cm
19[21:22]cm

Striped jersey

This jersey is easy to make in reversed stocking stitch and rib and there is very little shaping with the straight rib neckline.

Sizes

To fit 81[86:91:97]cm/32[34:36:38]in bust
Length to shoulder, 67[68:69:70]cm/26½[26¾: 27¼:27½]in
Sleeve seam, 48cm/19in
The figures in [] refer to the 86/34, 91/36 and 97cm/38in sizes respectively

You will need

7[8:8:9]×40g balls of Sirdar Wash 'n' Wear Double Crepe (55% Bri-Nylon, 45% acrylic) in main colour A
2[2:3:3] balls each of same in contrast colours B and C
One pair 3mm/No 11 needles
One pair 3¾mm/No 9 needles

Tension

24 sts and 32 rows to 10cm/4in over st st worked on 3¾mm/No 9 needles

Back

With 3mm/No 11 needles and A cast on 96[102:108:114] sts.
Work in K1, P1 rib for 9cm/3½in.
Next row (inc row) K2[4:8:10] sts, (inc in next st, K3) 23 times, inc in next st, K1[5:7:11].
120[126:132:138] sts.
Change to 3¾mm/No 9 needles.
Beg with a P row work in reverse st st in a stripe sequence of 2 rows B, 2 rows A, 2 rows C; 4 rows A.
Cont in patt without shaping until work measures 47cm/18½in from beg, ending with a Ws row.

Shape armholes

Cast off 12 sts at beg of next 2 rows. 96[102:108:114] sts.
Cont in patt without shaping until armholes measure 14[15:16:17]cm/5[5½:6:6½]in from beg, ending with 2 rows in B or C. Break off B and C.
Next row (Rs) P one row in A.
Next row (inc row) P3[6:9:12], (inc in next st, P5) 15 times, inc in next st, P2[5:8:11]. 112[118:124:130] sts.

Left: The loose fitting sleeves of this jersey are created by increasing into every stitch at the cuff.

alternative colourways

Yoke

Change to 3mm/No 11 needles.
Work 6cm/2¼in K1, P1 rib.
Cast off in rib.

Front

Work as given for back.

Sleeves

With 3mm/No 11 needles and A cast on 46[48:50:52] sts.
Work 9cm/3½in in K1, P1 rib.
Next row (inc row) Inc in each st to end of row. 92[96:100:104] sts.
Change to 3¾mm/No 9 needles.
Beg with a P row work in reverse st st in stripes as given for back until sleeve measures 48cm/19in from beg. Place a marker at both ends of last row.

Cont in st st until work measures 53cm/20¾in from beg.
Cast off loosely.

To make up

Press pieces with a warm iron over a damp cloth, omitting ribbing. Join shoulder seams for 5cm/2in. Set in sleeves. Join side and sleeve seams. Press seams.

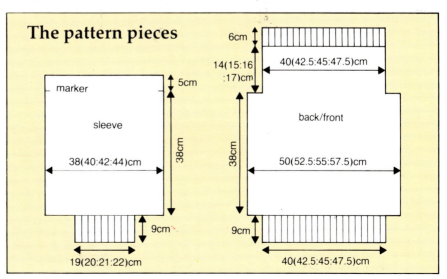

The pattern pieces

marker

sleeve

38(40:42:44)cm

5cm

38cm

9cm

19(20:21:22)cm

6cm

14(15:16:17)cm

40(42.5:45:47.5)cm

back/front

50(52.5:55:57.5)cm

38cm

9cm

40(42.5:45:47.5)cm

Cable pattern coat

This three-quarter length coat in reversed stocking stitch with twisted stitch panels combines warmth with casual elegance. Full sleeves are caught in at the cuffs with a neat rib to echo the stand-up collar.

Sizes

To fit 84 [94]cm/33 [37]in bust
Length to shoulder, 78 [80]cm/
 31 [31½]in
Sleeve seam, 45cm/17¾in
 adjustable
The figures in [] refer to the 94cm/
 37in size only

You will need

21 [23]×50g balls of Phildar
 Kadischa (75% acrylic, 25% wool)
One pair 6mm/No 4 needles
One pair 7mm/No 2 needles
One 7mm/No 2 crochet hook
One button

Tension

13 sts and 18 rows to 10cm/4in over patt worked on 7mm/No 2 needles

Back

With 7mm/No 2 needles cast on 78 [85] sts.
1st row (Rs) P3, *K second st on left-hand needle then K first st and sl them off needle tog – **called cr2**, P5, rep from * to last 5 sts, cr2, P3.
2nd row K3, *P2, K5, rep from * to last 5 sts, P2, K3.
These 2 rows form patt. Cont in patt until work measures 30cm/11¾in from beg, ending with a Ws row.

Shape panels

Next row P3 *cr2, P2, P2 tog, P1, rep from * to last 5 sts, cr2, P3.
68[74] sts.
Next row K3, *P2, K4, rep from * to last 5 sts, P2, K3.
Cont in patt as now set until work measures 56cm/22in from beg, ending with a Ws row.

Shape armholes

Keeping patt correct, cast off at beg of next and every row 3[4] sts twice, 2 sts twice and one st 4 times. 54[58] sts.
Cont without shaping until armholes measure 22 [24]cm/8¾ [9½]in from beg, ending with Ws row.

Shape shoulders

Cast off 7[8] sts at beg of next 4 rows. Cast off rem 26 sts.

Left front

With 7mm/No 2 needles cast on 38 [42] sts.
1st row (Rs) P3, *cr2, P5, rep from * to last 7 [4] sts, cr2, P5 [2] sts.
2nd row K5 [2] sts, *P2, K5, rep from * to last 5 sts, P2, K3.
Cont in patt as now set until work measures 30cm/11¾in from beg ending with a Ws row.

Shape panels

Next row P3, *cr2, P2, P2 tog, P1, rep from * to last 7[4] sts, cr2, P5[2] sts. 34[37] sts.

Next row K5[2] sts, *P2, K4, rep from * to last 5 sts, P2, K3.
Cont in patt as now set until work measures same as back to underarm, ending with a Ws row.

Shape armhole

Cast off at beg of next and every alt row 3[4] sts once, 2 sts once and one st twice. 27[29] sts.
Cont without shaping until armhole measures 18 [20]cm/7 [8¼]in from beg, ending with a Rs row.

Shape neck

Cast off at beg of next and every alt row 6 sts once, 3 sts once, 2 sts once and one st twice, ending with a Ws row.

Shape shoulder

Cast off at beg of next and foll alt row 7[8] sts twice.

Right front

With 7mm/No 3 needles cast on 38 [42] sts.
1st row (Rs) P5[2] sts, *cr2, P5, rep from * to last 5 sts, cr2, P3.
2nd row K3, *P2, K5, rep from * to last 7[4] sts, P2, K5[2] sts.
Cont in patt as now set until work measures 30cm/11¾in from beg, ending with a Ws row.

Shape panels

Next row P5[2] sts, *cr2, P2, P2 tog, P1, rep from * to last 5 sts, cr2, P3.
34[37] sts.
Cont in patt as now set and complete to match left front, reversing all shaping.

Sleeves

With 6mm/No 4 needles cast on 27 [29] sts.
1st row (Rs) P1, *K1, P1, rep from * to end.
2nd row K1, *P1, K1, rep from * to end.
Rep these 2 rows for 6cm/2¼in ending with a 1st row.

Small size only

Next row (inc row) K2, *inc 1 by picking up loop and K tbl, K2, inc 1, K1, rep from * 7 times more, inc 1, K1. 44 sts.

Medium size only

Next row (inc row) K1, *inc 1 by picking up loop and K tb1, K2, (inc 1, K1) twice, rep from * 6 times

The pattern pieces

15[17]cm
38[43]cm
sleeve
39cm
34[38]cm
6cm
21[22]cm

20cm
22[24]cm
11[12]cm
42[44]cm
52[57]cm
56cm
74[76]cm
left front
back
62[67]cm

more. 50 sts.

Both sizes

Change to 7mm/No 2 needles.
1st row (Rs) P3, *cr2, P4, rep from * to last 5 sts, cr2, P3.
2nd row K3, *P2, K4, rep from * to last 5 sts, P2, K3.
Cont in patt as now set, inc one st at each end of 21st and every foll 20th row until there are 50[56] sts.
Cont without shaping until sleeve measures 45cm/17¾in from beg, or required length to underarm, ending with a Ws row.

Shape top

Cast off at beg of next and every row 3[4] sts twice and 2 sts twice. Dec one st at each end of next and foll 7[9] alt rows, ending with a Ws row. Cast off at beg of next and every row 2 sts 4 times, 3 sts twice and 10 sts once.

Neckband

Join shoulder seams. With Rs of work facing and 6mm/No 4 needles, pick up and K55 [57] sts evenly round neck. Beg with a 2nd row, work in K1, P1 rib as given for cuff for 7cm/2¾in. Cast off in rib.

To make up

Do not press as this will flatten patt. Sew in sleeves. Join side and sleeve seams.

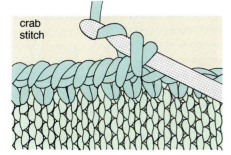

Front edges With Rs of left front edge facing and 7mm/No 2 hook, work one row of dc down front edge. Do not turn but work another row of dc back along same edge – **called crab st**. Work up right front edge in same way, making a button loop 4 sts from beg of last row by making 4ch, miss 3dc, 1dc into each dc to end. Sew on button to left front.

Right: This casual coat is light and warm and looks stunning worn with trousers for brisk country walks.

Fair Isle cardigan

The knitters of the Scottish Isles who are renowned for their skill at blending colours were probably not the originators of the art. Examples of Arabian coloured knitting indicate that it was well known by 450AD. The Moors brought the craft to Europe when they invaded Spain in the 8th century. The story goes that a ship of the Spanish Armada was wrecked on Fair Isle and the patterns on the jerseys of the dead sailors were copied by the islanders. One of the patterns is still called the Armada Cross.

Traditionally, Fair Isle patterns used natural wools that were hand dyed in muted shades of similar colours.

This cardigan has the same clever use of colour as an authentic Fair Isle pattern, but more contrasting colours are used in a smart, new design. The striking feature is the collar with multi-coloured fringing. Moss stitch has been used for the collar and cuffs to make an interesting effect. Extra instructions explain how the pattern can be adapted to a simple V neck.

Sizes

To fit 86 [91:97]cm/34 [36:38]in bust
Length to shoulder, 60 [61:62]cm/ 23½ [24:24½]in
Sleeve seam, 46cm/18in
The figures in [] refer to 91/36 and 97cm/38in sizes respectively

You will need

4 [5:5] x 50g balls of 3 Suisses Suizetta 4 ply (85% Acrylic, 15% wool) in main colour A
1 [2:2] x 50g balls of contrast colour B
1 x 50g ball each of contrast colours C, D, E, F, G and H
One 2¾mm/No 12 circular needle, 80cm/32in long
One 3¼mm/No 10 circular needle, 80cm/32in long
One pair 2¾mm/No 12 needles
One pair 3¼mm/No 10 needles
6 buttons

Tension

28 sts and 36 rows to 10cm/4in over st st and 28 sts and 28 rows to 10cm/4in over Fair Isle on 3¼mm/ No 10 needles

Left: A finely knitted Fair Isle cardigan with multi-coloured fringing to add zest

Back and fronts

(worked in one piece)
With 2¾mm/No 12 circular needle and A cast on 253 [265:277] sts.
Work 4cm/1½in moss st. Change to 3¼mm/No 10 circular needle.
Beg with a K row cont in st st and patt from chart until work measures 40cm/ 15¾in from beg, ending with a P row.

Divide for armholes

Next row Keeping patt correct throughout, K56 [59:62] sts, cast off 12 sts, K117 [123:129] sts, cast off 12 sts, K56 [59:62] sts.
Cont on last 56 [59:62] sts for left front.
Next row P to end.
Next row Cast off 2 sts, K to end.
Next row P to end.
Next row K1, K2 tog, K to end.
Rep last 2 rows 6 [7:8] times more, then P one row. 47 [49:51] sts.

Shape front edge

Next row K to last 3 sts, sl 1, K1, psso, K1.
Next row P to end.
Rep last 2 rows until 27 [28:29] sts rem. Cont without shaping until armhole measures 20 [21:22]cm/7¾ [8¼: 8¾]in from beg, ending with a P row.

Shape shoulder

Cast off at beg of next and every alt row 7 sts 3 times and 6 [7:8] sts once.
With Ws of work facing, rejoin yarn to 117 [123:129] sts for back and P to end.
Cast off 2 sts at beg of next 2 rows.
Next row K1, K2 tog, K to last 3 sts, sl 1, K1, psso, K1.
Next row P to end.
Rep last 2 rows 6 [7:8] times more. 99 [103:107] sts. Cont without shaping until armholes measure same as front to shoulder, ending with a P row.

Shape shoulders

Cast off at beg of next and every row 7 sts 6 times and 6 [7:8] sts twice. If making collar leave rem 45 [47:49] sts on holder for centre back neck. If making neckband, cast off.
With Ws of work facing, rejoin yarn to rem 56 [59:62] sts for right front and complete to match left front, reversing all shaping.

Sleeves

With 2¾mm/No 12 needles and A cast on 55 [59:63] sts. Work 4cm/1½in moss st. Change to 3¼mm/No 10 needles.
Beg with K row cont in st st patt from chart, starting on 43rd row.
Working extra sts into patt when possible, inc one st at each end of 7th

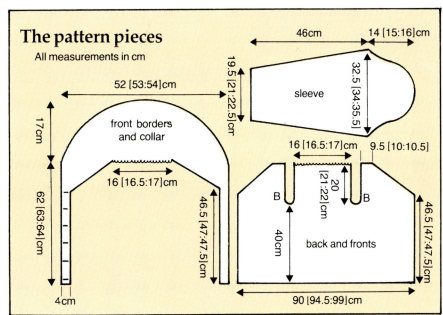

The pattern pieces

All measurements in cm

52 [53:54]cm

17cm

front borders and collar

16 [16.5:17]cm

62 [63:64]cm

4cm

19.5 [21:22.5]cm

46cm

14 [15:16]cm

sleeve

32.5 [34:35.5]

46.5 [47:47.5]cm

16 [16.5:17]cm

9.5 [10:10.5]

20 [21:22]cm

B

B

40cm

back and fronts

46.5 [47:47.5]cm

90 [94.5:99]cm

and every foll 6th row until there are 91 [95:99] sts.

Cont without shaping until sleeve measures about 46cm/18in from beg, ending with a P row and same patt row as at underarm on body.

Shape top

Cast off 6 sts at beg of next 2 rows. Dec one st at each end of next and every alt row as given for back until 59 [61:63] sts rem, ending with a P row.

Cast off at beg of next and every row

Chart for pattern rows

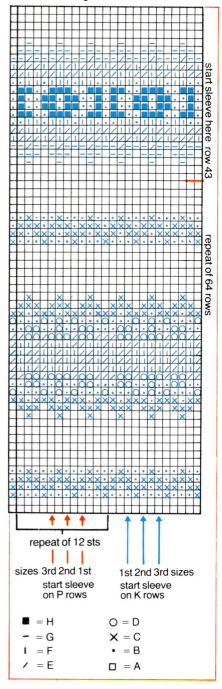

repeat of 12 sts

sizes 3rd 2nd 1st
start sleeve
on P rows

1st 2nd 3rd sizes
start sleeve
on K rows

start sleeve here row 43

repeat of 64 rows

■ = H	O = D
— = G	✕ = C
I = F	• = B
╱ = E	☐ = A

2 sts 10 times, 3 sts 4 times and 4 sts 4 times. Cast off rem 11 [13:15] sts.

Front borders and collar

Left front border

With 2¾mm/No 12 needles and A cast on 13 sts. Work in moss st until border is same length as front to shaping, ending with a Ws row. **. Inc one st at beg of next and every alt row until border measures same as front edge to shoulder, ending at shaped edge. Break off yarn and leave sts on holder.

Tack border in place along front edge and mark positions for buttons with pins, first pin in centre of welt and 6th pin about 2cm/¾in below beg of shaping, with 4 more evenly spaced between.

Right front border

With 2¾mm/No 12 needles and A cast on 13 sts. Work 2cm/¾in moss st ending with a Ws row.

Next row (buttonhole row) Moss st 5, cast off 3 sts, moss st to end.

Next row Moss st 5, cast on 3 sts, moss st to end.

Cont in moss st making buttonholes as markers are reached then cont until border, when slightly stretched, measures same as left front border to beg of shaping, ending with a Ws row. **

Inc one st at end of next and every alt row until border measures same as left front border, ending at straight edge.

Collar

Next row Moss st across sts of right front border, P across back neck sts

Above: The magic of Fair Isle is the way colours blend and melt together. Sketch

on holder, beg at shaped edge moss st across sts of left front border on holder.

Cont in moss st across all sts for 7cm/2¾in. Cast off at beg of next and every row 2 sts 36 times and 3 sts 12 times. Cast off rem sts.

Neckband

If collar is not required, cont in moss st on both borders from ** without shaping until borders reach to centre back neck. Cast off, join ends.

A sketch of the collarless version.

To make up

Do not press. Join shoulder seams. Set in sleeves. Join sleeve seams. Sew on front borders and collar, matching up right-front border with the left-front border which is already tacked in place. Alternatively sew on front borders and neckband only. From rem yarn cut lengths approx 15cm/6in long. Take 4 strands tog in colours as required and knot them into fringe round edge of collar. Sew on buttons.

your own colour combinations on graph paper before trying them out in knitting.

Look-alike slipovers in authentic Fair Isle

Well worth a second look, these attractive slipovers in traditional patterns and colours can be knitted to match – or in the same colours but different patterns.

The patterns have already been handed down over several centuries and such is their timeless appeal they will never date. So, your slipovers need not be discarded with the next fashion trend but can be among the treasured mainstays of your wardrobe for many years to come.

If you have a favourite Fair Isle pattern, you can use it to knit these slipovers. Count how many stitches and rows your pattern is worked over and, provided it corresponds to one of the charts given overleaf, substitute your own chart, working the colours in the sequence given.

Sizes

To fit 81 [86:91:97:102:107]cm/ 32 [34:36:38:40:42]in bust/chest
Length to shoulder 58 [60:63:65:67:69] cm/22¾ [23½:24¾:25½:26½:27¼]in
The figures in [] refer to 86/34, 91/36, 97/38, 102/40 and 107cm/42in sizes respectively

Below: These slipovers are machine washable and will keep their shape well.

Chart A

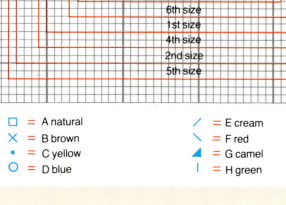

24 stitch pattern repeat
3rd size
6th size
1st size
4th size
2nd size
5th size

Chart B

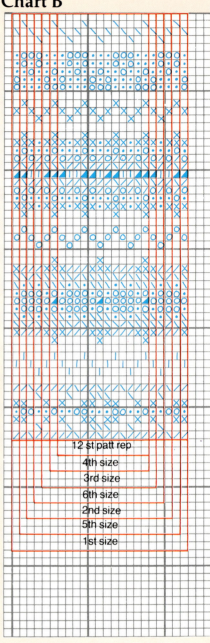

12 st patt rep
4th size
3rd size
6th size
2nd size
5th size
1st size

	= A natural		= E cream
✕	= B brown	⟋ = F red
•	= C yellow	◢ = G camel
○	= D blue	∣ = H green

The pattern piece

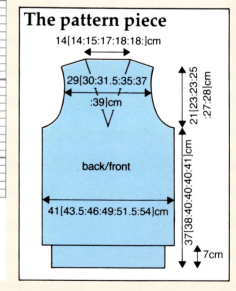

14[14:15:17:18:18:]cm

29[30:31.5:35:37 :39]cm

21[23:23:25 :27:28]cm

back/front

37[38:40:40:40:41]cm

41[43.5:46:49:51.5:54]cm

7cm

You will need

Version A 2 [3:3:3:4:4]×50g balls of Patons Clansman 4 ply (100% wool) in main colour A
1 [1:1:1:1:2] balls of same in contrast colour B
1 [1:1:1:1:1] ball of same in each of contrast colours C, D, E, F, G and H

Version B 2 [3:3:3:4:4]×50g balls of same in main colour A
1 [1:1:1:1:1] ball of same in each of contrast colours B, C, E, F, G and H
1 [1:1:1:1:2] balls of same in contrast colour D
One pair 2¾mm/No 12 needles
One pair 3¼mm/No 10 needles

Tension

28 sts and 36 rows to 10cm/4in over st st and 32 sts and 32 rows to 10cm/4in over Fair Isle patt worked on 3¼mm/No 10 needles

Note

When working patt from charts carry yarn not in use loosely across back of work. Read all K rows from right to left and all P rows from left to right.

Back version A

With 2¾mm/No 12 needles and A cast on 114 [122:128:136:144:150] sts. Work 7cm/2¾in K1, P1 rib, ending with a Rs row.

1st, 2nd, 3rd and 5th sizes only
Next row (inc row) Rib 1 [5:1:2] sts, *pick up loop lying between needles and K tbl – **called M1**, rib 7 sts, rep from * to last 1 [5:1:2] sts, M1, rib to end. 131 [139:147:165] sts.

4th and 6th sizes only
Next row (inc row) Rib 3 [4] sts, *pick up loop lying between needles and K tbl – **called M1**, rib 6 sts, M1, rib 7 sts, rep from * to last 3 [3] sts, M1, rib to end. 157 [173] sts.

All sizes

Change to 3¼mm/No 10 needles. Join in and break colours as required. Work in patt from chart A, rep the 24 patt sts 5 [5:6:6:6:7] times, and K the first 5 [9:1:6:10:2] and last 6 [10:2:7:11:3] sts and P the first 6 [10:2:7:11:3] and last 5 [9:1:6:10:2] sts as indicated. Cont in patt until back measures 37 [38:40:40:40:41]cm/14½ [15:15¾:15¾:15¾:16¼]in from beg, or length to underarm, ending on a Ws row.**

Shape armholes

Keeping patt correct throughout, cast off 5 sts at beg of next 2 rows. Dec one st at each end of next 7 [9:11:7:9:11] rows, then at each end of every foll alt row until 93 [97:101:113:119:125] sts rem. Cont without shaping until armholes measure 21 [22:23:25:27:28]cm/8¼ [8¾:9:9¾:10¾:11]in from beg, ending with a Ws row.

Shape shoulders

Cast off at beg of next and every row 8 [9:9:10:10:11] sts 4 times and 8 [8:8:9:11:12] sts twice.
Leave rem 45 [45:49:55:57:57] sts on holder for back neck.

Front version A

Work as given for back to **.
Keeping patt correct throughout shape armholes and divide for neck as foll:
Next row Cast off 5 sts, patt 58 [62:66:71:75:79] sts, K2 tog, turn and leave rem sts on holder. Complete left shoulder on these 59 [63:67:72:76:80] sts. Work one row.
Dec one st at armhole edge on next 7 [9:11:7:9:11] rows then on every foll alt row 7 [7:7:10:9:8] times more, *at the same time* dec one st at neck edge on next and every alt row until 34 [35:36:41:44:47] sts rem.
Cont dec one st at neck edge only on every foll 4th row from previous dec until 24 [26:26:29:31:34] sts rem. Cont without shaping until front measures same as back to shoulder, ending with a Ws row.

Shape shoulder

Cast off at beg of next and every alt row 8 [9:9:10:10:11] sts twice and 8 [8:8:9:11:12] sts once.
With Rs of work facing sl centre st on to safety pin for centre front neck, rejoin appropriate colour to rem sts, sl 1, K1, psso, patt to end. Complete to match first side reversing all shapings.

Back and front version B

Work as given for version A but working in patt from chart B instead of chart A, rep the 12 patt sts 10 [11:12:13:13:14] times, and K the first 5 [3:1:0:4:2] and last 6 [4:2:1:5:3] sts and P the first 6 [4:2:1:5:3] and last 5 [3:1:0:4:2] sts as indicated.

Above: The pattern is worked on the back and front of traditional slipovers. If preferred the back could be knitted plain.

Neckband (both versions)

Join right shoulder seam. With Rs facing, 2¾mm/No 12 needles and A, pick up and K66 [70:74:82:90:94] sts down left side of neck, K centre st from safety pin and mark this with coloured thread, pick up and K66 [70:74:82:90:94] sts up right side of neck then K across 45 [45:49:55:57:57] sts from back neck holder dec 5 sts evenly. 173 [181:193:215:233:241] sts.
1st row (Ws) *P1, K1, rep from * to within 2 sts of marked centre st, P2 tog, P centre st, P2 tog tbl, **K1, P1, rep from ** to end.
2nd row *K1, P1, rep from * to within 2 sts of marked centre st, P2 tog tbl, K centre st, P2 tog, **K1, P1, rep from ** to last st, K1.
Rep these 2 rows 3 times more then 1st row again.
Cast off in rib, dec at either side of centre st as before.

Armbands (both versions)

Join left shoulder and neckband seam. With Rs facing, 2¾mm/No 12 needles and A, pick up and K128 [136:144:160:176:184] sts evenly round armhole. Work 9 rows K1, P1 rib. Cast off in rib.

To make up (both versions)

Press each piece under a damp cloth with a warm iron, omitting ribbing. Join side and armband seams. Press seams.

Icelandic jerseys

These jerseys are knitted totally in the round, including the sleeves and yoke, eliminating any making up except for grafting the few stitches at the underarms.

If you find grafting difficult, cast off these underarm stitches instead of transferring to waste yarn and seam them together to complete the jersey.

Sizes

To fit 81 [87:91:97:102:107]cm/32 [34:36:38:40:42]in bust/chest
Length to back neck, 61 [64:64:66: 66:68]cm/24 [25¼:25¼:26:26:26¾]in
Sleeve seam, 44 [44:45:46:48:50]cm/ 17¼ [17¼:17¾:18:19:19¾]in
The figures in [] refer to the 87/34, 91/36, 97/38, 102/40 and 107cm/42in sizes respectively

You will need

7 [7:8:8:9:9]×50g balls of Alafoss Lopi Lyng (100% wool) in main colour A
2 [2:2:2:2:2] balls of same in contrast colour B
1 [1:1:1:1:1] ball of same in contrast colour C
One 4½mm/No 7 circular needle 80cm/30in long
One 6½mm/No 3 circular needle 80cm/30in long
One 6½mm/No 3 circular needle 40cm/16in long
Set of four 4½mm/No 7 needles pointed at both ends

Left: Achieve your own look with the use of colour. These two jerseys are both worked in similar tones, but one has a dark shade used as main colour and the other a lighter shade.

Tension

14 sts and 19 rows to 10cm/4in over st st worked on 6½mm/No 3 needles

Jersey body

With 4½mm/No 7 circular needle 80cm/30in long and A cast on 108 [112:118:120:126:138] sts. Mark beg of round with coloured thread and work in rounds.
Work 10 rounds K1, P1 rib.
Change to 6½mm/No 3 circular needle 80cm/30in long.
Next round (inc round) K9 [7:10:5: 8:8] sts, *pick up loop lying between needles and K tbl – **called M1**, K18 [14:14:10:10:11]sts, rep from * 4 [6:6:10:10:10] times more, M1, K to end. 114 [120:126:132:138:150] sts.
Cont in st st and work 11 rounds from chart 1. Break off B and C.
Cont in st st with A only until work measures 38 [39:41:42:43:45]cm/15 [15½:16:16½:17:17½]in from beg, ending 4 [4:4:4:5:5] sts *before* end of last round to divide for underarms.

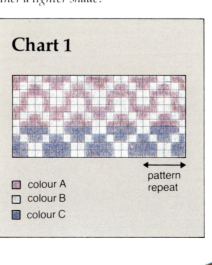

Chart 1

| colour A |
| colour B |
| colour C |

pattern repeat

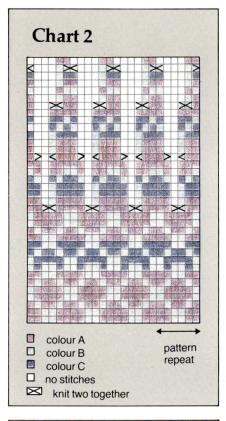

Chart 2

- ▨ colour A
- ☐ colour B
- ▨ colour C
- ☐ no stitches
- ⊠ knit two together

pattern repeat

Above: The subtle blend of neutral shades form the attractive yoke on this jersey. All shaping is done within the pattern rows as shown on the chart.

Divide for underarms

Next round K first 9 [9:9:9:10:10] sts, sl these sts on to separate length of thread for underarm, K57 [60:63:66: 69:75] sts, sl last 9 [9:9:9:10:10] of these sts on to another thread for underarm, K rem 48 [51:54:57:59: 65] sts.
Leave work for time being.

Sleeves

With set of four 4½mm/No 7 needles and A cast on 30 [30:30:30: 32:34] sts. Mark beg of round with coloured thread and work in rounds.
Work 10 rounds K1, P1 rib.
Change to 6½mm/No 3 circular needle 40cm/16in long.
Next round (inc round) K4 [4:4:4:2: 4] sts, *M1, K2 [2:2:2:3:2] sts, rep from * 10 [10:10:10:8:12] times more, M1, K to end. 42 [42:42:42:42:48] sts.
Cont in st st and work 11 rounds from chart 1. Break off B and C.
Cont in st st with A only inc one st at beg and end of every foll 8th round until there are 50 [50:50:50: 56:56] sts.
Cont without shaping until sleeve

measures 44 [44:45:46:48:50]cm/17¼ [17¼:17¾:18:19:19¾]in from beg, ending 4 [4:4:4:5:5] sts *before* end of last round for underarm.
Sl next 8 [8:8:8:10:10] sts on to a separate length of thread. 42 [42:42: 42:46:46] sts.

Yoke

With Rs of work facing, 6½mm/No 3 circular needle 80cm/30in long and A, join body and sleeves for yoke.
Next round K42 [42:42:42:46:46] sts from first sleeve, K48 [51:54:57:59: 65] sts across body for front of jersey, K42 [42:42:42:46:46] sts from 2nd sleeve and K48 [51:54:57:59: 65] sts across body for back of jersey. 180 [186:192:198:210:222] sts.
Cont in st st and work 36 rounds from chart 2, dec where indicated with A in 16th, 23rd and 30th rounds and with C in 35th round.

Neckband

Change to set of four 4½mm/No 7 needles and A only. Work 8 [8:8:8: 9:10] rounds K1, P1 rib.
Cast off knitwise.

To make up

Press lightly under a damp cloth with a warm iron.
Darn in all ends. Graft or seam underarm sts of sleeves to body.

The pattern pieces

41[43:45:47:49:53]cm

yoke stitches

front/back

34[35:37:38:39:41]cm

4cm

38[40:42:43:45:49]cm

18[18:18:18:20:20]cm

yoke stitches

half width of sleeve

40[40:41:42:44:46]cm

15[15:15:15: 15:17]cm

4cm

10[10:10:10:11:12]cm

note: these pieces are knitted in the round

Jacquard yoked jersey

Sizes

To fit 86 [91:97]cm/34 [36:38] in bust
Length to shoulder, 60 [61:62]cm/
23½ [24:24½]in
Sleeve seam, 47cm/18½in
The figures in [] refer to the 91cm/
36in and 97cm/38in sizes
respectively

You will need

9 [10:10]×50g balls of Sunbeam
  Trophy Double Knitting (80%
wool, 20% nylon) in main colour A
1 ball of same in each of 5 contrast
  colours B, C, D, E and F
One pair 3mm/No 11 needles
One pair 3¾mm/No 9 needles
Set of four 3mm/No 11 needles
Set of four 3¾mm/No 9 needles

Tension

24 sts and 32 rows to 10cm/4in over
plain st st worked on 3¾mm/No 9
needles

Back

With 3mm/No 11 needles and A cast
on 106 [114:118] sts.
1st row (Rs) K2, *P2, K2, rep from *
to end.
2nd row P2, *K2, P2, rep from* to end.
Rep these 2 rows for 6cm/2¼in,
ending with a 2nd row and inc
3 [1:3] sts evenly in last row.
109 [115:121] sts.
Change to 3¾mm/No 9 needles.
Beg with a K row cont in st st until
work measures 35cm/13¾in from
beg, ending with a P row.
Join in colours as required and cont
in st st, working first 12 rows from
jacquard chart.

Jacquard chart

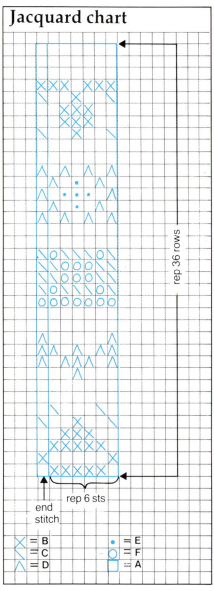

rep 36 rows

rep 6 sts

end stitch

×= B
＝C
∧= D

•= E
○= F
□= A

Shape armholes

Cont in patt from chart, cast off 4 sts at beg of next 2 rows.
Next row K1, K2 tog, patt to last 3 sts, sl 1, K1, psso, K1.
Next row Patt to end.
Working throughout in patt from chart, rep these 2 rows until 37 [39:41] sts rem, ending with a Ws row, noting that after completing the 36 rows once, the first 5 rows of next rep should be worked using F instead of B, then on foll rep go back to B.
Leave sts on holder.

Front

Work as given for back, shaping armholes until 57 [59:61] sts rem, ending with a Ws row.

Shape neck

Next row K1, K2 tog, patt 19 sts, turn and leave rem sts on holder. Complete left shoulder first.
Next row Cast off 3 sts, patt to end.
Next row K1, K2 tog, patt to end.
Next row Cast off 2 sts, patt to end.
Next row K1, K2 tog, patt to last 2 sts, K2 tog.
Next row Patt to end.
Rep last 2 rows 4 times more, then cont to dec at armhole edge only on every alt row until 2 sts rem, ending with a Ws row. Cast off.
Return to rem sts on holder, leave first 13 [15:17] sts for centre front neck, rejoin yarn to rem sts, patt to last 3 sts, sl 1, K1, psso, K1.
Next row Patt to end.

Next row Cast off 3 sts, patt to last 3 sts, sl 1, K1, psso, K1.
Complete to match first side, reversing all shapings.

Sleeves

With 3mm/No 11 needles and A cast on 50 [54:58] sts. Work 8cm/3¼in rib as given for back, ending with a 1st row.
Next row (inc row) Rib 7 [9:5] sts, *pick up loop lying between sts and K tbl – called M1, rib 3 [3:4] sts, rep from * 11 times more, M1, rib 7 [9:5] sts. 63 [67:71] sts.
Change to 3¾mm/No 9 needles. Beg with a K row cont in st st, inc one st at each end of 9th [5th:1st] row and every foll 8th row until there are 85 [91:97] sts. Cont without shaping until sleeve measures 43cm/17in from beg, ending with a P row.
Join in colours as required and cont in st st, working first 12 rows from jacquard chart.

Shape top

Cont in patt from chart, cast off 4 sts at beg of next 2 rows.
Cont dec as given for back at each end of next and every alt row until 13 [15:17] sts rem, changing to F instead of B on first 5 rows of second patt rep and ending with a Ws row. Leave sts on holder.

Neckband

Join raglan seams with Rs facing and invisible seam, taking care to

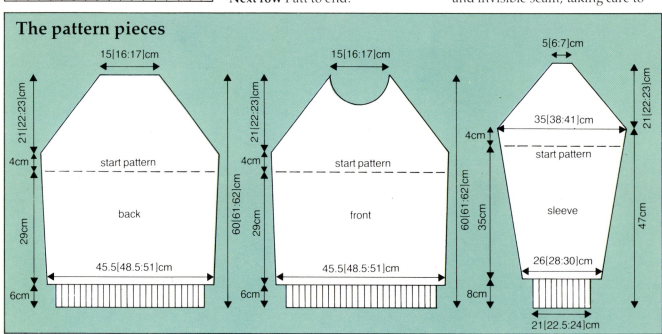

The pattern pieces

15[16:17]cm
21[22:23]cm
4cm
start pattern
29cm
back
45.5[48.5:51]cm
6cm

15[16:17]cm
21[22:23]cm
4cm
start pattern
60[61:62]cm
29cm
front
45.5[48.5:51]cm
6cm

5[6:7]cm
21[22:23]cm
4cm
35[38:41]cm
start pattern
60[61:62]cm
35cm
sleeve
47cm
26[28:30]cm
8cm
21[22.5:24]cm

match patt exactly.

With Rs of work facing, set of four 3mm/No 11 needles and A, K across sts of right sleeve, back neck and left sleeve K2 tog at each seam, pick up and K17 sts down left front neck, K across front neck sts on holder, pick up and K17 sts up right front neck. 108 [116:124] sts.

Work 8cm/3¼in in rounds of K2, P2 rib. Change to set of four 3¾mm/No 9 needles. Cont in rib until neckband measures 20cm/7¾in from beg. Cast off very loosely.

To make up

Block out each piece and press under a damp cloth with a warm iron.

Join side and sleeve seams, using oversewing for rib, invisible method for side seams and back st for sleeve seams. Press seams.

Below: Blocking and pressing the pieces of this jersey will improve the final appearance of the finished garment.
Inset: Samples knitted in the same yarn as the jersey to give you an idea of some alternative colourways.

Guernseys for a man or woman

These jerseys include many of the traditional guernsey features, such as mock side seams and underarm and neck gussets, and the sleeves are knitted from the shoulder to the cuff. To make the garments easier to knit they have been worked on circular needles, instead of sets of needles, and divided at the armholes.

Sizes

To fit 86[91:97:102]cm/34 [36:38:40]in bust/chest loosely
Length to shoulder, 63 [65:67:69]cm/ 24¾ [25½:26½:27¼]in
Sleeve seam, 46 [47:48:49]cm/ 18 [18½:19:19¼]in, adjustable
The figures in [] refer to the 91/36, 97/38 and 102cm/40in sizes respectively.

You will need

16 [17:18:19] × 50g balls of Emu guernsey (100% wool)
One pair 2¾mm/No 12 needles
One pair 3mm/No 11 needles
One 2¾mm/No 12 circular needle 100cm/40in long
One 3mm/No 11 circular needle 100cm/40in long
Set of four 2¾mm/No 12 needles pointed at both ends
Set of four 3mm/No 11 needles pointed at both ends
One cable needle

Tension

28 sts and 36 rows to 10cm/4in over st st worked on 3mm/No 11 needles

Body

With 2¾mm/No 12 needles cast on 127 [135:143:151] sts by casting on 2 sts, lift 2nd st over 1st and off needle. Cast on 2 more sts and rpt until total is reached. Work 7cm/2¾in in g st ending with a Ws row. Break off yarn and leave sts. Work second piece in same way. Do not break yarn.

Join body

Change to 2¾mm/No 12 circular needle and cont working in rounds to underarm.
Next round Inc in first st, K to end across second piece, cont across first piece and inc in first st, K to end. Join into a circle taking care not to twist sts. 256 [272:288:304] sts.
Work 6 rounds K2, P2 rib.
Change to 3mm/No 11 circular needle. Commence mock side seams.
1st round *P1, K127 [135:143:151] sts, rep from * once more.
2nd round K to end.
Rep these 2 rounds until work measures 38cm/15in from beg, ending with a 1st round.

Shape underarm gusset

1st round *Pick up loop lying between sts and K tbl – called M1, K1, M1, K127 [135:143:151] sts, rep from * once more.
2nd round K to end.
3rd round *M1, K3, M1, K127 [135:143:151] sts, rep from * once more.
Cont inc in this way on every alt round until there are 292 [308:324:340] sts, ending with an inc round.

Divide for armholes

Next row K19 sts and sl these sts on to a thread for gusset, K127[135:143:151] sts, turn and leave rem sts on spare needle. Complete front first. K 4 rows g st, inc one st in centre of last row on 1st and 2nd sizes only, and dec one st in centre of last row on 3rd and 4th sizes only. 128 [136:142:150] sts.
Next row (Ws) K1, (K1, P1) 1 [3:1:3] times, (K2, P5) 1 [1:2:2] times, *K2, P6, K2, P13, K2, P6, K2*, P42, rep from * to *, (P5, K2) 1 [1:2:2] times, (P1, K1) 1 [3:1:3] times, K1.
Sts are now set for yoke patt. Cont in patt.

Yoke

1st row P1, (P1, K1) 1 [3:1:3] times, (P2, K5) 1 [1:2:2] times, *P2, K6, P2, (K6, P1, K6 noting that these 13 sts are 1st row of heart patt, see page 77), P2, K6, P2*, (K6, P2, K12, P2, K12, P2, K6 noting that these 42 sts are 1st row of Sheringham herringbone and diamond patt, see page 77), rep from * to*, (K5, P2) 1[1:2:2] times, (K1, P1) 1[3:1:3] times, P1.
2nd row K1, (K1, P1) 1 [3:1:3] times, (on 3rd and 4th sizes only K2, P4, K1), on all sizes K3, P4, *K2, P6, K2, work 2nd row of heart patt, K2, P6, K2*, work 2nd row of Sheringham patt, rep from * to *, P4, K3, (on 3rd and 4th sizes only K1, P4, K2), on all sizes (P1, K1) 1 [3:1:3] times, K1.
3rd row P1, (P1, K1) 1 [3:1:3] times, (on 3rd and 4th sizes only P2, K3, P1, K1), on all sizes P2, K1, P1, K3, *P2, sl next 3 sts on to cable needle and hold at back of work, K3 then K3 from cable needle – **called C6B**, P2, work 3rd row of heart patt, P2, sl next 3 sts on to cable needle and hold at front of work, K3 then K3 from cable needle – **called C6F**, P2*, work 3rd row of Sheringham patt, rep from * to *, K3, P1, K1, P2, (on 3rd and 4th sizes only K1, P1, K3, P2), on all sizes (K1, P1) 1 [3:1:3] times, P1.
4th row K1, (K1, P1) 1 [3:1:3] times, (K2, P2, K1, P2) 1 [1:2:2] times, *K2, P6, K2, work 4th row of heart patt, K2, P6, K2*, work 4th row of Sheringham patt, rep from * to *, (P2, K1, P2, K2) 1 [1:2:2] times, (P1, K1) 1 [3:1:3] times, K1.
5th row P1, (P1, K1) 1 [3:1:3] times,

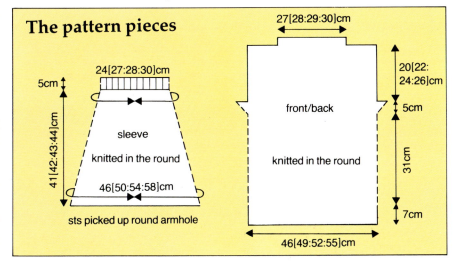

The pattern pieces

27[28:29:30]cm

24[27:28:30]cm

5cm

sleeve
knitted in the round

46[50:54:58]cm

41[42:43:44]cm

sts picked up round armhole

20[22: 24:26]cm

front/back
knitted in the round

5cm

31cm

7cm

46[49:52:55]cm

(on 3rd and 4th sizes only P2, K1, P1, K3), on all sizes P2, K3, P1, K1, *P2, K6, P2, work 5th row of heart patt, P2, K6, P2*, work 5th row of Sheringham patt, rep from * to *, K1, P1, K3, P2, (on 3rd and 4th sizes only K3, P1, K1, P2), on all sizes (K1, P1) 1 [3:1:3] times, P1.
6th row K1, (K1, P1) 1 [3:1:3] times, (on 3rd and 4th sizes only K3, P4), on all sizes K2, P4, K3, *P6, K2, work 6th row of heart patt, K2, P6*, K2, work 6th row of Sheringham patt, K2, rep from * to *, K3, P4, K2, (on 3rd and 4th sizes only P4, K3), on all sizes (P1, K1) 1 [3:1:3] times, K1.
Working 16 row rep of heart patt and Sheringham patt, rep the last 6 rows until armholes measure 20 [22:24:26]cm/7¾ [8¾:9½:10¼]in from beg, ending with a Ws row.

Shape shoulders
Cast off 26 [29:31:34] sts at beg of next 2 rows. Leave rem 76 [78:80:82] sts on holder.
Return to sts on spare needle, with Rs facing rejoin yarn, K first 19 sts of gusset and leave on a thread, K to end.
Complete back to match front.

Neckband
Join shoulder seams. Sl back and front neck sts on to 2 needles from a set of 2¾mm/No 12 needles.
With Rs of work facing and 2¾mm/ No 12 needles, pick up and K1 st from neck edge of left shoulder seam, turn and P1.
Next row K1, then K1 from needle holding front neck sts, turn.
Next row P2, then P1 from needle holding back neck sts, turn.
Next row K3, then K1 from needle holding front neck sts, turn.
Cont in this way until there are 11 sts on needle. Break off yarn and leave sts for time being.
Rep at other side of neck, reading front for back and vice versa. Do not break off yarn.
With Rs of work facing and set of four 2¾mm/No 12 needles K across all sts round neck, inc one st at centre back and centre front. 156 [160:164:168] sts.
Cont in rounds of K2, P2 rib for 5cm/2in. Cast off loosely in rib.

Sleeves
With Rs of work facing and set of

four 3mm/No 11 needles, K across 19 sts of one underarm gusset, pick up and K110 [120:132:142] sts round armhole.
1st round K19 sts, P to end.
2nd round Sl 1, K1, psso, K15, K2 tog, K to end.
3rd round K17, P to end.
4th round Sl 1, K1, psso, K13, K2 tog, K to end.
5th round K to end.
Working in st st, cont to dec in the same way at each side of gusset sts on next and every alt round until 113 [123:135:145] sts rem, ending with a plain round.
18th round Sl 1, K2 tog, psso, K to end. 111 [121:133:143] sts.
19th round K to end.
20th round P1, K to end.
Rep 19th and 20th rounds twice more.
Next round K1, sl 1, K1, psso, K to

Above: This guernsey yoke includes the Fife heart and Sheringham herringbone and diamond patterns.

last 2 sts, K2 tog.
Next round As 20th.
Keeping mock seam st correct throughout, cont to dec in this way on every 6th [6th:5th:5th] round until 67 [75:77:85] sts rem.
Cont without shaping until sleeve measures 41 [42:43:44]cm/16¼ [16½:17:17¼]in from end of gusset dec 3 [7:5:9] sts evenly in last round, or required length less 5cm/2in. Change to set of four 2¾mm/No 12 needles. Cont in rounds of K2, P2 rib for 5cm/2in. Cast off loosely in rib.

To make up
Press very lightly under a damp cloth with a warm iron.

Sheringham herringbone and diamond pattern

The pattern is worked on multiples of 28 stitches plus 14 stitches and makes an all-over pattern for a yoke. The double moss stitch diamonds are flanked by herringbones.

1st row (Rs) *K6, P2, K12, P2, K6, rep from * to last 14 sts, K6, P2, K6.

2nd row *P6, K2, P12, K2, P6, rep from * to last 14 sts, P6, K2, P6.

3rd row *K5, P1, K2, P1, K9, P2, K2, P2, K4, rep from * to last 14 sts, K5, P1, K2, P1, K5.

4th row *P4, K1, P4, K1, P8, K2, P2, K2, P4, rep from * to last 14 sts, P4, K1, P4, K1, P4.

5th row *K3, P1, K6, P1, K5, (P2, K2) 3 times, rep from * to last 14 sts, K3, P1, K6, P1, K3.

6th row *P2, K1, P8, K1, P4, (K2, P2) 3 times, rep from * to last 14 sts, P2, K1, P8, K1, P2.

7th row *K1, P1, K10, P1, K1, (P2, K2) 3 times, P2, rep from * to last 14 sts, K1, P1, K10, P1, K1.

8th row *K1, P12, K1, (K2, P2) 3 times, K2, rep from * to last 14 sts, K1, P12, K1.

9th row *K6, P2, K8, (P2, K2) 3 times, rep from * to last 14 sts, K6, P2, K6.

10th row *P6, K2, P8, (K2, P2) 3 times, rep from * to last 14 sts, P6, K2, P6.

11th and 12th row As 3rd and 4th.

13th row *K3, P1, K6, P1, K9, P2, K6, rep from * to last 14 sts, K3, P1, K6, P1, K3.

14th row *P2, K1, P8, K1, P8, K2, P6, rep from * to last 14 sts, P2, K1, P8, K1, P2.

15th row *K1, P1, K10, P1, K15, rep from * to last 14 sts, K1, P1, K10, P1, K1.

16th row *K1, P12, K1, P14, rep from * to last 14 sts, K1, P12, K1. These 16 rows form the pattern.

Fife heart pattern

The pattern is worked on multiples of 16 stitches plus 3 stitches. It is a romantic little motif and makes a useful filler between larger patterns.

1st row (Rs) *P1, K1, P1, K6, P1, K6, rep from * to last 3 sts, P1, K1, P1.

2nd row *K1, P1, K1, P5, K3, P5, rep from * to last 3 sts, K1, P1, K1.

3rd row *P1, K1, P1, K4, P2, K1, P2, K4, rep from * to last 3 sts, P1, K1, P1.

4th row *K1, P1, K1, P3, K2, P3, K2, P3, rep from * to last 3 sts, K1, P1, K1.

5th row *P1, K1, P1, K2, P2, K5, P2, K2, rep from * to last 3 sts, P1, K1, P1.

6th row *(K1, P1) twice, K2, P3, K1, P3, K2, P1, rep from * to last 3 sts, K1, P1, K1.

7th row *(P1, K1) twice, P2, K2, P3, K2, P2, K1, rep from * to last 3 sts, P1, K1, P1.

8th row *K1, P1, K1, P2, K4, P1, K4, P2, rep from * to last 3 sts, K1, P1, K1.

9th row *P1, K1, P1, (K3, P2) twice, K3, rep from * to last 3 sts, P1, K1, P1.

10th row *K1, P1, K1, P13, rep from *to last 3 sts, K1, P1, K1.

11th row *P1, K1, P1, K13, rep from * to last 3 sts, P1, K1, P1.

12th row As 10th.

Rep 11th and 12th rows twice more. These 16 rows form the pattern.

Traditional woollen guernseys

Knit this lovely guernsey in hard-wearing traditional guernsey wool. It features the well-known side vents on the welts and underarm gussets. The yoke is patterned with cables, plaits and a zigzag brocade pattern. Try using the special method of casting on for a really neat finish – see Professional Touch.

Sizes

To fit 81 [86:91:97:102:107]cm/32 [34:36:38:40:42]in bust/chest
Length to shoulder, 61 [63:65:67:69:71]cm/24 [24¾:25½:26½:27¼:28]in
Sleeve seam, 45 [46:47:48:49:50]cm/17¾ [18:18½:19:19¼:19¾]in
The figures in [] refer to the 86/34, 91/36, 97/38, 102/40 and 107cm/42in sizes respectively

You will need

7 [8:8:9:9:10]×100g balls of Poppleton's Guernsey 5 ply (100% wool)
One pair 2¾mm/No 12 needles
One pair 3mm/No 11 needles
One 2¾mm/No 12 circular needle 80cm/30in long
One 3mm/No 11 circular needle 80cm/30in long
Set of four 2¾mm/No 12 needles pointed at both ends
Set of four 3mm/No 11 needles pointed at both ends
Cable needle

Tension

28 sts and 36 rows to 10cm/4in over st st worked on 3mm/No 11 needles

Cable panel A

Worked over 6 sts.
1st row K6.
2nd row P6.
3rd and 4th rows As 1st and 2nd.
5th row Sl next 3 sts on to cable needle and hold at back of work, K3 then K3 from cable needle.
6th row As 2nd.
7th and 8th rows As 1st and 2nd.
These 8 rows form the pattern.

Cable panel B

Worked over 6 sts.
Work first 4 rows as cable panel A.

Left: No making up is necessary when knitting guernseys the traditional way.

5th row Sl next 3 sts on to cable needle and hold at front of work, K3 then K3 from cable needle.
6th to 8th rows As cable panel A.
These 8 rows form the pattern.

Cable panel C

Worked over 6 sts.
Work first 2 rows as cable panel A.
3rd row Sl first 2 sts on to cable needle and hold at back of work, K2 then K2 from cable needle, K2.
4th row As 2nd.
5th and 6th rows As 1st and 2nd.
7th row K2, sl next 2 sts on to cable needle and hold at front of work, K2 then K2 from cable needle.
8th row As 2nd.
These 8 rows form the pattern.

Zig-zag panel

Worked over 14 sts.
1st row K10, P2, K2.
2nd row P2, K2, P10.
3rd row K9, P2, K3.
4th row P3, K2, P9.
5th row K8, P2, K4.
6th row P4, K2, P8.
7th row K7, P2, K5.
8th row P5, K2, P7.
9th row K6, P2, K6.
10th row P6, K2, P6.
11th row K5, P2, K7.
12th row P7, K2, P5.
13th row K4, P2, K8.
14th row P8, K2, P4.
15th row K3, P2, K9.
16th row P9, K2, P3.
17th row K2, P2, K10.
18th row P10, K2, P2.
19th to 32nd rows Work 15th, 16th,

13th, 14th, 11th, 12th, 9th, 10th, 7th, 8th, 5th, 6th, 3rd and 4th rows. These 32 rows form the pattern.

Ladder panel

Worked over multiples of 6 sts plus 2.
1st row P2, (K4, P2) number of times given.
2nd row K2, (P4, K2) number of times given.
3rd row As 1st.
4th row K to end.
These 4 rows form the pattern.

Body

With 2¾mm/No 12 needles cast on 117 [125:133:141:149:157] sts. Work 7cm/2¾in g st, ending with a Ws row and inc one st in centre and one st at each end of last row. 120 [128:136:144:152:160] sts.
Break off yarn and leave these sts for time being.
Work a 2nd piece in same way but do not break off yarn.

Join welts

Change to 2¾mm/No 12 circular needle.
Next round *K1, (P2, K2) to last 3 sts of 2nd piece, P2, K1, then rep from * across first piece which was left. 240 [256:272:288:304:320] sts.
Work 6 more rounds in rib as set. Change to 3mm/No 11 circular needle.
1st round K to end.
2nd round *P1, K119 [127:135:143:151:159] sts, rep from * once more. Rep last 2 rounds until work

---

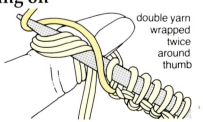

measures 38cm/15in from beg, ending with a 2nd round.

Shape underarm gusset
1st round *Pick up loop lying between sts and K tbl – **called M1**, K1, M1, K119 [127:135:143:151: 159] sts, rep from * once more.
2nd round K to end.
3rd round *M1, K3, M1, K119 [127: 135:143:151:159] sts, rep from * once more.
Cont to inc in this way on every alt round until there are 276 [292:308: 324:340:356] sts, ending with an inc round.

Divide for armholes
Next row Using 3mm/No 11 needle, K19 and sl these sts on to a thread for gusset, K119 [127:135: 143:151: 159] sts, turn and cont on these sts for back, leaving rem sts on circular needle.
K 5 rows, inc 3 sts in last row. 122 [130:138:146:154:162] sts.

Yoke
1st row P0 [0:2:2:0:0], (K2, P2) 3 [4:3:4:4:5] times, P2, K6 for cable panel A, P2, (K4, P2) 2 [2:3:3:4:4] times for ladder panel, K6 for cable panel A, P2, (K10, P2, K2) for 1st row of zig-zag panel, P2, K6 for cable panel C, P2, (K2, P2, K10) for 17th row of zig-zag panel, P2, K6 for cable panel B, P2, (K4, P2) 2 [2:3:3:4:4] times for ladder panel, K6 for cable panel B, P2, (P2, K2) 3 [4:3:4: 4:5] times, P0 [0:2:2:0:0].
2nd row K0 [0:2:2:0:0], (P2, K2) 3 [4:3:4:4:5] times, K2, P6, work 2nd row of ladder panel over next 14 [14:20:20:26:26] sts, P6, K2, work 18th row of zig-zag panel over next 14 sts, K2, P6, K2, work 2nd row of

zig-zag panel over next 14 sts, K2, P6, work 2nd row of ladder panel over next 14 [14:20:20:26:26] sts, P6, K2, (K2, P2) 3 [4:3:4:4:5] times, K0 [0:2:2:0:0].
3rd row K0 [0:2:2:0:0], (P2, K2) 3 [4:3:4:4:5] times, P2, K6, work 3rd row of ladder panel over next 14 [14:20:20:26:26] sts, K6, P2, work 3rd row of zig-zag panel over next 14 sts, P2, work 6 sts as 3rd row of cable panel C, P2, work 15th row of zig-zag panel over next 14 sts, P2, K6, work 3rd row of ladder panel over next 14 [14:20:20:26:26] sts, K6, P2, (K2, P2) 3 [4:3:4:4:5] times, K0 [0:2:2:0:0].
4th row P0 [0:2:2:0:0], (K2, P2) 3 [4:3:4:4:5] times, K2, P6, K14 [14:20: 20:26:26] for ladder panel, P6, K2, work 16th row of zig-zag panel over next 14 sts, K2, P6, K2, work 4th row of zig-zag panel over next 14 sts, K2, P6, K14 [14:20:20:26:26] for ladder panel, P6, K2, (P2, K2) 3 [4:3:4:4:5] times, P0 [0:2:2:0:0].
These 4 rows form rep of double moss st patt at each end. Keeping these correct and working other panels as set, cont until armholes measure 17 [19:21:23:25:27]cm/6¾ [7½:8¼:9:9¾:10¾]in from beg, ending with a Ws row.

Shape neck and shoulders
Next row K24 [27:30:33:36:39] sts, turn and leave rem sts on spare needle.
K 1 row, (P 2 rows, K 2 rows) twice then P 1 row and leave sts on a separate thread to graft.
Return to sts on spare needle, sl first 74 [76:78:80:82:84] sts on to holder for back neck, rejoin yarn to rem sts and K to end.
Complete to match first shoulder.

Return to sts which were left for front, rejoin yarn and work to match back but working one row less on shoulders before leaving sts to graft.

Sleeves
Graft shoulder seams, or cast off and seam tog.
With Rs of work facing, set of four 3mm/No 11 needles K across 19 sts of one underarm gusset, pick up and K108 [116:124:132:140:148] sts round armhole.
1st round K19, P to end.
2nd round Sl 1, K1, psso, K15, K2 tog, K to end.
3rd round K17, P to end.
4th round Sl 1, K1, psso, K13, K2 tog, K to end.
5th round K15, P to end.
Working all sts in st st, cont to dec at each side of gusset on every alt round as before until 3 sts rem in gusset, ending with a plain round.
Next round Sl 1, K2 tog, psso, K to end.
Next round K to end.
Next round P1, K to end.
Rep last 2 rounds once more, then first of them again.
Next round P1, sl 1, K1, psso, K to last 2 sts, K2 tog.
Keeping the P st on every alt round correct throughout, cont to dec on every 6th [6th:5th:5th:5th:4th] round until 65 [69:73:77:81:85] sts rem.
Cont without shaping until sleeve measures 40 [41:42:43:44:45]cm/15¾ [16¼:16½:17:17¼:17¾]in from *end* of gusset, or 5cm/2in less than final length required, dec 5 [5:5:9:9:9] sts evenly in last round.
Change to set of four 2¾mm/No 12 needles. Work 5cm/2in rounds of K2, P2 rib. Cast off loosely in rib.

Neckband
With Rs of work facing and set of four 2¾mm/No 12 needles, *K across back neck sts dec 2 sts over each cable, pick up and K12 sts along side of neck, rep from * round front and along other side of neck. 160 [164:168:172:176:180] sts.
Work 5cm/2in rounds of K2, P2 rib. Cast off in rib.

To make up
Press lightly under a damp cloth with a warm iron, taking care not to flatten yoke patt.

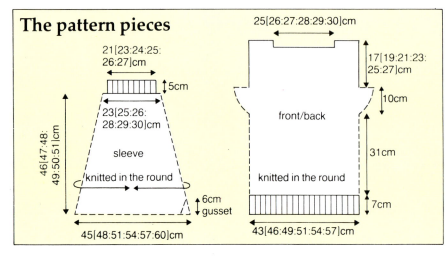

The pattern pieces

21[23:24:25: 26:27]cm

↕5cm

23[25:26: 28:29:30]cm

sleeve

knitted in the round

46[47:48: 49:50:51]cm

↕6cm gusset

45[48:51:54:57:60]cm

25[26:27:28:29:30]cm

17[19:21:23: 25:27]cm

front/back

10cm

31cm

knitted in the round

7cm

43[46:49:51:54:57]cm

Traditional Aran jersey

Bobble and rib pattern are worked up the centre of this jersey with a panel of zigzag and bobble pattern worked up each side.

The pattern panels are separated by narrow cables and all extra stitches at the sides worked in Aran moss stitch. An attractive pattern called the Tree of Life is used to form the rib at the bottom of the jersey, the end of the sleeves and at the neck, which is folded back to give a neat edge.

Sizes

To fit 86–91 [97–102:107–112]cm/34–36 [38–40:42–44]in bust/chest
Length to shoulder, 60 [63:66]cm/23½ [24¾:26]in
Sleeve seam, 44 [46:48]cm/17¼ [18:19]in
The figures in [] refer to the 97–102/38–40 and 107–112cm/42–44in sizes respectively

You will need

17 [18:19]×50g balls of Hayfield Brig Aran (100% wool)
One pair 3¾mm/No 9 needles
One pair 4½mm/No 7 needles
One cable needle

Tension

18 sts and 24 rows to 10cm/4in over Aran moss st patt worked on 4½mm/No 7 needles

Back

With 3¾mm/No 9 needles cast on 97 [109:121] sts.
1st row (Rs) K2, *P3, K3 tbl, P3, K3, rep from * to last 11 sts, P3, K3 tbl, P3, K2.
Beg with a 2nd row cont in tree of life welt as given on page 83 for 8 rows. Rep these 8 rows once more then first row again.
Next row (inc row) Patt 5 [9:10] sts as 2nd row, *pick up loop lying between needles and K tbl – **called M1**, patt 8 [13:34] sts as 2nd row, rep from * 10 [6:2] times more, M1, patt 4 [9:9] sts as 2nd row. 109 [117:125] sts.
Change to 4½mm/No 7 needles.

Right: Square set-in sleeves and a simple neckline minimize the shaping.

Commence patt.
1st row (Rs) (K1, P1) 5 [7:9] times for Aran moss stitch (see opposite), P2, K6, work 14 sts as 1st row of zigzag and bobble patt (see opposite), K6, P2, work 29 sts as 1st row of bobble and rib patt (see opposite), P2, K6, work 14 sts as 13th row of zigzag and bobble patt (see opposite), K6, P2, (P1, K1) 5 [7:9] times for Aran moss stitch.
2nd row (P1, K1) 5 [7:9] times for Aran moss st, K2, P6, work 14 sts as 14th row of zigzag and bobble patt, P6, K2, work 29 sts as 2nd row of bobble and rib patt, K2, P6, work 14 sts as 2nd row of zigzag and bobble patt, P6, K2, (K1, P1) 5 [7:9] times for Aran moss st.
3rd row (P1, K1) 5 [7:9] times for Aran moss st, P2, sl next 3 sts on to cable needle and hold at back of work, K3 then K3 from cable needle – **called C6B**, work 14 sts as 3rd row of zigzag and bobble patt, C6B, P2, work 29 sts as 3rd row of bobble and rib patt, P2, C6B, work 14 sts as 15th row of zigzag and bobble patt, C6B, P2, (K1, P1) 5 [7:9] times from Aran moss st.
4th row (K1, P1) 5 [7:9] times for Aran moss st, K2, P6, work 14 sts as 16th row of zigzag and bobble patt, P6, K2, work 29 sts as 4th row of bobble and rib patt, K2, P6, work 14 sts as 4th row of zigzag and bobble patt, P6, K2, (K1, P1) 5 [7:9] times for Aran moss st.
Keeping all patt panels correct as now set and sts at each end in Aran moss st, work C6B on each cable panel on every 6th row and cont in patt until work measures 39 [40:41]cm/15¼ [15¾:16¼] in from beg, ending with a Ws row.

Shape armholes
Keeping patt correct throughout, cast off 10 [12:14] sts at beg of next 2 rows. 89 [93:97] sts.
Cont without shaping until armholes measure 21 [23:25]cm/8¼ [9:9¾]in from beg, ending with a Ws row.

Shape shoulders
Cast off at beg of next and every row 7 [7:8] sts 4 times and 7 [8:8] sts 4 times.
Leave rem 33 sts on holder for centre back neck.

Front
Work as given for back until armholes measure 14 [16:18] cm/5½ [6¼:7]in from beg, ending with a Ws row.

Shape neck
Next row Patt 37 [39:41] sts, turn and leave rem sts on spare needle. Complete left shoulder first.
Cast off at neck edge 2 sts at beg of next and foll alt row, then dec one st at beg of foll 5 alt rows. 28 [30:32] sts.
Cont without shaping until armhole measures same as back to shoulder, ending with a Ws row.

Shape shoulder
Cast off at beg of next and foll alt rows 7 [7:8] sts twice and 7 [8:8] sts twice.
With Rs of work facing sl first 15 sts on spare needle on to holder, rejoin yarn to rem sts and patt to end. Complete right shoulder to match left, reversing all shapings.

Sleeves
With 3¾mm/No 9 needles cast on 49[49:61] sts. Work 17 rows welt patt as given for back.
Next row (inc row) Patt 3 [8:5] sts as 2nd row, *M1, patt 6 [3:17] sts as 2nd row, rep from *6 [10:2] times more, M1, patt 4 [8:5] sts as 2nd row. 57 [61:65] sts.
Change to 4½mm/No 7 needles. Commence patt.
1st row (Rs) (K1, P1) 2 [3:4] times for Aran moss st, P2, K6, P2, work 29 sts as 1st row of bobble and rib patt, P2, K6, P2, (P1, K1) 2 [3:4] times for Aran moss st.
Keeping patt correct as now set, work C6B on the two cable panels on 3rd and every foll 6th row, *at the same time* inc one st at each end.of the 7th and every foll 8th [7th:6th] row until there are 77 [85:93] sts, working extra sts into Aran moss st.
Cont without shaping until sleeve measures 44 [46:48]cm/17¼ [18:19]in from beg. Place a marker at each end of last row.
Work a further 14 [16:18] rows, noting that these rows are set into armhole. Cast off loosely.

Neckband
Join right shoulder seam. With Rs of work facing and 3¾mm/No 9 needles pick up and K21 sts down left front neck, K across front neck sts, pick up and K20 sts up right front neck, then K across back neck sts, working K5, (K2 tog, K5) 4 times. 85 sts.
Next row P4, *(P1 tbl, K3) twice, P1 tbl, P3, rep from * to last 9sts, (P1 tbl, K3) twice, P1.
Next row P3, *K3 tbl, P3, K3, P3, rep from * to last 10 sts, K3 tbl, P3, K3, P1.
Starting and ending rows as now set, rep the 2nd to 8th rows of welt patt once.
Next row P to end.
Next row K1, *P3, K3, rep from * to end.
Next row *P3, K3, rep from * to last st, P1.
Rep last 2 rows 3 times more. Cast off in patt.

To make up
Do not press as this will flatten patt. Join left shoulder and neckband seam. Sew in sleeves, sewing lst row of sleeves from markers to cast off sts at armholes. Join side and sleeve seams. Fold neckband in half to Ws and sl st down.

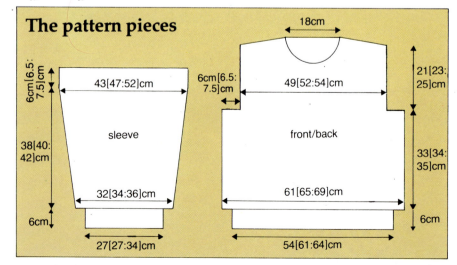

The pattern pieces

sleeve
43[47:52]cm
6cm[6.5:7.5]cm
38[40:42]cm
32[34:36]cm
6cm
27[27:34]cm

18cm
front/back
6cm[6.5:7.5]cm
49[52:54]cm
21[23:25]cm
33[34:35]cm
6cm
61[65:69]cm
54[61:64]cm

Tree of life welt pattern

This wide rib pattern has three knit stitches alternating with a tree of life. It is worked on multiples of 12 stitches plus one stitch.

1st row (Rs) K2, *P3, K3 tbl, P3, K3, rep from * to last 11 sts, P3, K3 tbl, P3, K2.

2nd row P2, *K3, P3 tbl, K3, P3, rep from * to last 11 sts, K3, P3 tbl, K3, P2.

3rd row K2, *P2, sl next st on to cable needle and hold at back of work, K1 tbl from left-hand needle then P1 from cable needle – **called C2B**, K1 tbl, sl next st on to cable needle and hold at front of work, P1 from left-hand needle then K1 tbl from cable needle – **called C2F**, P2, K3, rep from * to last 11 sts, P2, C2B, K1 tbl, C2F, P2, K2.

4th row P2, *K2, (P1 tbl, K1) twice, P1 tbl, K2, P3, rep from * to last 11 sts, K2, (P1 tbl, K1) twice, P1 tbl, K2, P2.

5th row K2, *P1, C2B, P1, K1 tbl, P1, C2F, P1, K3, rep from * to last 11 sts, P1, C2B, P1, K1 tbl, P1, C2F, P1, K2.

6th row P2, *K1, (P1 tbl, K2) twice, P1 tbl, K1, P3, rep from * to last 11 sts, K1, (P1 tbl, K2) twice, P1 tbl, K1, P2.

7th row K2, *C2B, P2, K1 tbl, P2, C2F, K3, rep from * to last 11 sts, C2B, P2, K1 tbl, P2, C2F, K2.

8th row P2, *(P1 tbl, K3) twice, P1 tbl, P3, rep from * to last 11 sts, (P1 tbl, K3) twice, P1 tbl, P2.

These 8 rows form the pattern.

Aran moss stitch

This traditional name is given to a simple double moss stitch. It is worked on multiples of 2 stitches plus one stitch.

1st row (Rs) K1, *P1, K1, rep from * to end.

2nd row P1, *K1, P1, rep from * to end.

3rd row As 2nd row.

4th row As 1st row.

These 4 rows form the pattern.

Bobble and rib pattern

An unusual Aran pattern combining a central triangle shape filled in with rib and bobbles, with panels of boble clusters on each side. It is worked over 29 stitches.

1st row (Rs) K5, P7, K2, (K1, P1, K1, P1, K1) all into next st, turn and K5, turn and P5, with point of left-hand needle lift 2nd, 3rd, 4th and 5th sts over first st on right-hand needle and off needle – **called MB**, K2, P7, K5.

2nd row P5, K7, P2, P1 tbl, P2, K7, P5.

3rd row K5, P6, sl next st on to cable needle and hold at back of work, K2 sts from left-hand needle then P1 from cable needle – **called C3BP**, K1 tbl, sl next 2 sts on to cable needle and hold at front of work, P1 from left-hand needle then K2 from cable needle – **called C3FP**, P6, K5.

4th row P5, K6, P2, K1, P1 tbl, K1, P2, K6, P5.

5th row K5, P5, sl next st on to cable needle and hold at back of work, K2 sts from left-hand needle then K1 tbl from cable needle – **called C3BK**, P1, K1 tbl, P1, sl next 2 sts on to cable needle and hold at front of work, K1 tbl from left-hand needle then K2 from cable needle – **called C3FK**, P5, K5.

6th row P5, K5, P2, (P1 tbl, K1) twice, P1 tbl, P2, K5, P5.

7th row K2, MB, K2, P4, C3BP, (K1 tbl, P1) twice, K1 tbl, C3FP, P4, K2, MB, K2.

8th row P5, K4, P2, (K1, P1 tbl) 3 times, K1, P2, K4, P5.

9th row K1, (MB, K1) twice, P3, C3BK, (P1, K1 tbl) 3 times, P1, C3FK, P3, K1, (MB, K1) twice.

10th row P5, K3, P2 (P1 tbl, K1) 4 times, P1 tbl, P2, K3, P5.

11th row K5, P2, C3BP, (K1 tbl, P1) 4 times, K1 tbl, C3FP, P2, K5.

12th row P5, K2, P2, (K1, P1 tbl) 5 times, K1, P2, K2, P5.

These 12 rows form the pattern.

Zigzag and bobble pattern

This pattern is said to represent a cliff path winding between boulders It is worked on multiples of 14 st stitches.

1st row (Rs) *P3, sl next 2 sts on to cable needle and hold at front of work, P1 from left-hand needle then K2 from cable needle – **called C3FP**, P8, rep from * to end.

2nd row *K8, P2, K4, rep from * to end.

3rd row *P4, C3FP, P7

4th row *K7, P2, K5

5th row *P5, C3FP, P6

6th row *K6, P2, K6

7th row *P6, C3FP, P5

8th row *K5, P2, K7

9th row *P7, C3FP, P4

10th row *K4, P2, K8

11th row *P5, (K into front and back of next st) twice, then K into front again, making 5 sts, turn and K5, turn and P5, then with point of left-hand needle lift 2nd, 3rd, 4th and 5th sts over first and off needle – **called MB**, P2, C3FP, P3.

12th row *K3, P2, K9.

13th row *P8, sl next st on to cable needle and hold at back of work, K2 from left-hand needle then P1 from cable needle – **called C3BP**, P3.

14th row As 10th row.

15th row *P7, C3BP, P4.

16th row As 8th row.

17th row *P6, C3BP, P5.

18th row As 6th row.

19th row *P5, C3BP, P6.

20th row As 4th row.

21st row *P4, C3BP, P7.

22nd row As 2nd row.

23rd row *P3, C3BP, P2, MB, P5.

24th row *K9, P2, K3.

These 24 rows form the pattern.

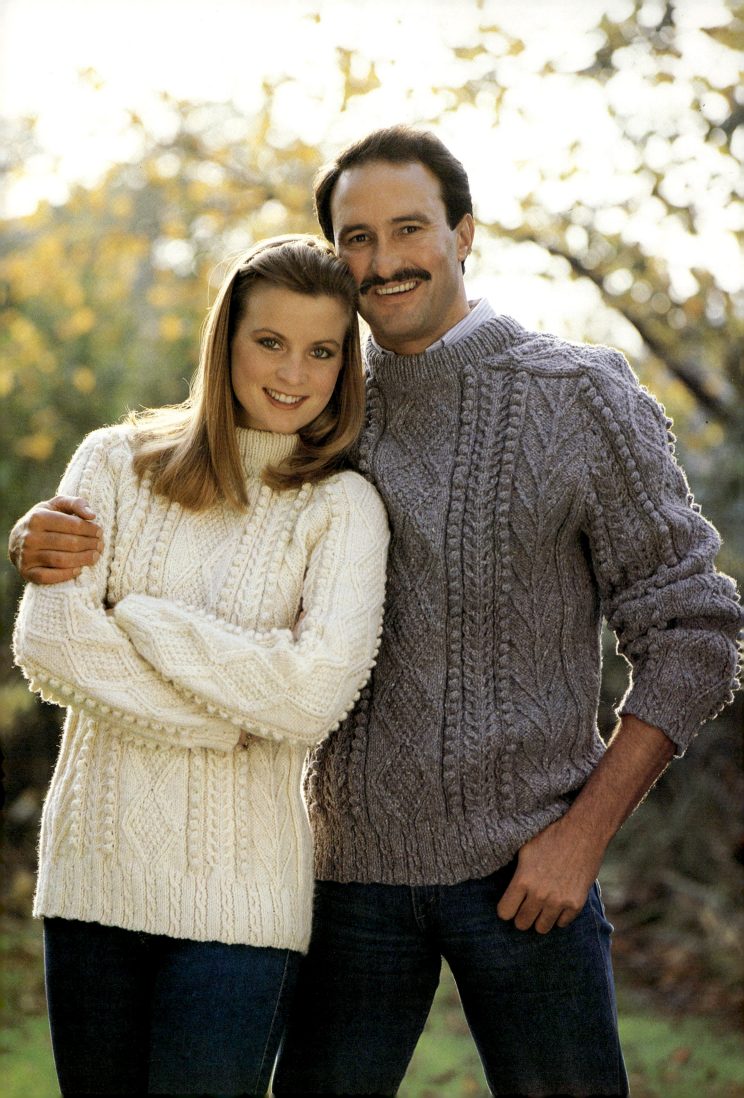

Aran sweaters

Aran sweaters traditionally come from the islands off the western coast of Ireland. These authentic jerseys are knitted in Aran wool with moss stitch diamonds on the centre panel of the body and sleeves, with panels of bobbles, lobster claw cables and the tree of life design on either side. The centre panel on the sleeves continues to form a saddle-top shoulder line. The sweaters are finished with a neat ribbed crew neck for comfort.

Sizes

To fit 86/91 [97/102]cm/
34/36 [38/40]in bust/chest
Length to shoulder 66 [70]cm/
26 [27½]in
Sleeve seam, 46 [48]cm/18 [19]in
The figures in [] refer to 97-102cm/
38-40in size only

You will need

21 [25] x 50g balls of Sunbeam Aran Knit or Aran Tweed
One pair 3¾mm/No 9 needles
One pair 4½mm/No 7 needles
Set of four 3¾mm/No 9 needles
1 cable needle

Tension

20 sts and 28 rows to 10cm/4in over st st worked on 4½mm/No 7 needles

Back

With 3¾mm/No 9 needles cast on 123 [139] sts. Commence rib.
1st row K3, *P1, (K1 tbl, P1) twice, K3, rep from * to end.
2nd row P3, *K1, (P1 tbl, K1) twice, P3, rep from * to end.
3rd and 4th rows As 1st and 2nd
5th row K3, *P1, sl next st on to cable needle and hold at front of work, K second st on left-hand needle then P first st and sl both sts off needle tog, K1 tbl from cable needle – **called cr3**, P1, K3, rep from * to end.
6th row As 2nd.
Rep these 6 rows twice more, then first 2 rows once more. Change to 4½mm/No 7 needles.
1st row (Rs) K3, (P1, (K1 tbl, P1) twice, K3) once [twice], *P8, K next 3

sts tbl, P8, **, K3, P2, K9, P2, K3, ***, P2, K7, (K1 tbl, P1) 3 times, K1 tbl, K7, P2, rep from ** to *** once, then from * to ** once, K3, (P1, (K1 tbl, P1) twice, K3) once [twice].
2nd row P3, (K1, (P1 tbl, K1) twice, P3) once [twice], *K8, P next 3 sts tbl, K8, **, P3, K2, P9, K2, P3, ***, K2, P7, (P1 tbl, K1) 3 times, P1 tbl, P7, K2, rep from ** to *** once, then from * to ** once, P3, (K1, (P1 tbl, K1) twice, P3) once [twice].
3rd row K3, (P1, cr3, P1, K3) once [twice], *P7, sl next st on to cable needle and hold at back of work, K1 tbl from left-hand needle then P1 from cable needle – **called tw2R**, K1 tbl, sl next st on to cable needle and hold at front of work, P1 from left-hand needle then K1 tbl from cable needle – **called tw2L**, P7, **, K3, P2, K9, P2, K3, ***, P2, K6, (tw2R) twice, K1, (tw2L) twice, K6, P2, rep from ** to *** once, then from * to ** once, K3, (P1, cr3, P1, K3) once [twice].
4th row Patt 11 [19] sts as 2nd row, *K7, (P1 tbl, K1) twice, P1 tbl, K7,** P3, K2, P9, K2, P3, ***, K2, P6, (P1 tbl, K1) twice, P1, (K1, P1 tbl) twice, P6, K2, rep from ** to *** once, then from * to ** once, patt 11[19]sts as 2nd row.
5th row Patt 11 [19] sts as 1st row, *P6, tw2R, P1, K1 tbl, P1, tw2L, P6, **, K1, K into front, back, front and back of next st making 4 sts, turn, sl 1, P3, turn, pass the 2nd, 3rd and 4th sts on left-hand needle over the first then K this st tbl – **called MB**, K1, P2, sl next 3 sts on to cable needle and hold at back of work, K1 from left-hand needle, K3 from cable

needle, K1 from left-hand needle, sl next st on to cable needle and hold at front of work, K3 from left-hand needle then K1 from cable needle – **called cable 9**, P2, K1, MB, K1, ***, P2, K5, (tw2R) twice, K1, P1, K1, (tw2L) twice, K5, P2, rep from ** to *** once, then from * to ** once, patt 11[19]sts as 1st row.
6th row Patt 11 [19] sts as 2nd row, *K6, (P1 tbl, K2) twice, P1 tbl, K6, **, patt 19 sts as 2nd row, ***, K2, P5, (P1 tbl, K1) twice, P1, K1, P1, (K1, P1 tbl) twice, P5, K2, rep from ** to *** once, then from * to ** once, patt 11 [19] sts as 2nd row.
7th row Patt 11 [19] sts as 1st row, *P5, tw2R, P2, K1 tbl, P2, tw2L, P5, **, patt 19 sts as 1st row, ***, P2, K4, (tw2R) twice, K1, (P1, K1) twice, (tw2L) twice, K4, P2, rep from ** to *** once, then from * to ** once, patt 11 [19] sts as 1st row.
8th row Patt 11 [19] sts as 2nd row, *K5, (P1 tbl, K3) twice, P1 tbl, K5, **, patt 19 sts as 2nd row, ***, K2, P4, (P1 tbl, K1) twice, (P1, K1) twice, P1, (K1, P1 tbl) twice, P4, K2, rep from ** to *** once, then from * to ** once, patt 11 [19] sts as 2nd row.
9th row Patt 11 [19] sts as 3rd row, *P4, tw2R, P3, K1 tbl, P3, tw2L, P4, **, patt 19 sts as 5th row, ***, P2, K3, (tw2R) twice, K1, (P1, K1) 3 times, (tw2L) twice, K3, P2, rep from ** to *** once, then from * to ** once, patt 11 [19] sts as 3rd row.
10th row Patt 11 [19] sts as 2nd row, *K4, (P1 tbl, K4) 3 times, **, patt 19 sts as 2nd row, ***, K2, P3, (P1 tbl, K1) twice, (P1, K1) 3 times, P1, (K1, P1 tbl) twice, P3, K2, rep from ** to *** once, then from * to ** once, patt 11

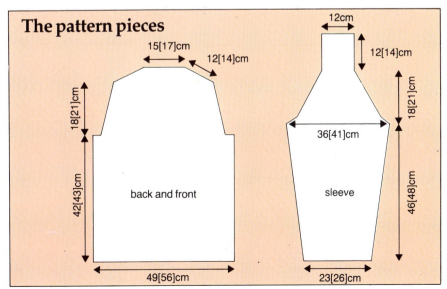

The pattern pieces

15[17]cm
12[14]cm
18[21]cm
42[43]cm
back and front
49[56]cm

12cm
12[14]cm
18[21]cm
36[41]cm
sleeve
46[48]cm
23[26]cm

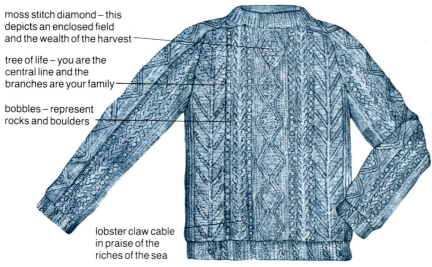

moss stitch diamond – this depicts an enclosed field and the wealth of the harvest

tree of life – you are the central line and the branches are your family

bobbles – represent rocks and boulders

lobster claw cable in praise of the riches of the sea

[19] sts as 2nd row.

11th row Patt 11 [19] sts as 1st row, *P3, tw2R, P4, K1 tbl, P4, tw2L, P3, **, patt 19 sts as 1st row, ***, P2, K2, (tw2R) twice, K1, (P1, K1) 4 times, (tw2L) twice, K2, P2, rep from ** to *** once, then from * to ** once, patt 11 [19] sts as 1st row.

12th row Patt 11 [19] sts as 2nd row, *K3, P1 tbl, (K5, P1 tbl) twice, K3, **, patt 19 sts as 2nd row, ***, K2, P2, (P1 tbl, K1) twice, (P1, K1) 4 times, P1, (K1, P1 tbl) twice, P2, K2, rep from ** to *** once, then from * to ** once, patt 11 [19] sts as 2nd row.

13th row Patt 11 [19] sts as 1st row, *P2, tw2R, P4, K next 3 sts tbl, P4, tw2L, P2, **, patt 19 sts as 5th row, ***, P2, K1, (tw2R) twice, K1, (P1, K1) 5 times, (tw2L) twice, K1, P2, rep from ** to *** once, then from * to ** once, patt 11 [19] sts as 1st row.

14th row Patt 11[19] sts as 2nd row, *K2, P1 tbl, K5, P next 3 sts tbl, K5, P1 tbl, K2, **, patt 19 sts as 2nd row, ***, K2, P1, (P1 tbl, K1) twice, (P1, K1) 5 times, P1, (K1, P1 tbl) twice, P1, K2, rep from ** to *** once, then from * to ** once, patt 11[19] sts as 2nd row.

15th row Patt as 3rd row to centre panel of 25 sts, P2, K1, sl next st on to cable needle and hold at front of work, K1 from left-hand needle then K1 tbl from cable needle – **called tw2LK**, tw2L, (P1, K1) 5 times, P1, tw2R, sl next st on to cable needle and hold at back of work, K1 tbl from left-hand needle then K1 from cable needle – **called tw2RK**, K1, P2, patt as 3rd row to end.

16th row Patt as 4th row to centre panel, patt centre 25 sts as 12th row, patt as 4th row to end.

17th row Patt 5th row to centre panel, P2, K2, tw2LK, tw2L, (P1, K1) 4 times, P1, tw2R, tw2RK, K2, P2, patt as 5th row to end.

18th row Patt as 6th row to centre panel, patt centre 25 sts as 10th row, patt as 6th row to end.

19th row Patt as 7th row to centre panel, P2, K3, tw2LK, tw2L, (P1, K1) 3 times, P1, tw2R, tw2RK, K3, P2, patt as 7th row to end.

20th row As 8th row.

21st row Patt as 9th row to centre panel, P2, K4, tw2LK, tw2L, (P1, K1) twice, P1, tw2R, tw2RK, K4, P2, patt as 9th row to end.

22nd row Patt as 10th row to centre panel, patt centre 25 sts as 6th row, patt as 10th row to end.

23rd row Patt as 11th row to centre panel, P2, K5, tw2LK, tw2L, P1, K1, P1, tw2R, tw2RK, K5, P2, patt as 11th row to end.

24th row Patt as 12th row to centre panel, patt centre 25 sts as 4th row, patt as 12th row to end.

25th row Patt as 13th row to centre panel, P2, K6, tw2LK, tw2L, P1, tw2R, tw2RK, K6, P2, patt as 13th row to end.

26th row Patt as 14th row to centre panel, patt centre 25 sts as 2nd row, patt as 14th row to end.

The 3rd to 26th rows form patt and are rep throughout. Cont in patt until back measures 42 [43]cm/16½ [17]in from beg, ending with a Ws row. Adjust length if required.

Shape armholes

Keeping patt correct, cast off at beg of next and every row 8 sts twice and 2[3] sts twice.

Dec one st at each end of next and every foll 4th row until 81[91] sts rem, then work one row ending with a Ws row.

Shape shoulders

Cast off at beg of next and every row 8[9] sts 4 times and 9[10] sts twice. Leave rem 31[35] sts on holder for neck.

Front

Work as given for back.

Sleeves

With 3¾mm/No 9 needles cast on 51 [59] sts. Work 13 rows rib patt as given for back.
14th row Patt 4[7] sts, *M1, P3, M1, P2[3] sts, rep from * 8[7] times more, patt 2 [4] sts. 69 [75] sts. Change to 4½mm/No 7 needles. Cont in Aran patt as foll:
1st row P0[1] st, K1[3] sts, P2, *K3, P2, K9, P2, K3, *, P2, K7, (K1 tbl, P1) 3 times, K1 tbl, K7, P2, rep from * to *, P2, K1[3] sts, P0[1] st.
2nd row K0[1] st, P1[3] sts, K2, *P3, K2, P9, K2, P3, *, K2, P7, (P1 tbl, K1) 3 times, P1 tbl, P7, K2, rep from * to *, K2, P1[3] sts, K0[1] st.
Cont in patt as now set, working centre panel with cable and bobble panels at each side as for back, inc one st at each end of 9th and every foll 8th row, working extra sts into welt patt, until there are 89[99] sts. Cont without shaping until sleeve measures 46 [48]cm/18 [19]in from beg, ending with a Ws row.

Shape top

Cast off at beg of next and every row 8 sts twice and 2[3] sts twice. Dec one st at each end of next and every alt row until 25 sts rem.
Cont in patt on these 25 sts for length of shoulder, ending with a Ws row. Leave sts on holder.

Neckband

Sew saddle top of sleeves to shoulders.
With set of four 3¾mm/No 9 needles and Rs of work facing, K across all sts on holders, K2 tog at each seam. 108 [116] sts.
Cont in rounds of K1, P1 rib for 6cm/2¼in. Cast off loosely in rib.

To make up

Do not press as this will flatten the patt. Sew in sleeves. Join side and sleeve seams.
Fold neckband in half to inside and sl st down.
Press seams only under a damp cloth with a warm iron.

Norwegian-type cardigan

This attractive Norwegian-style cardigan is knitted in a slightly fluffy yarn. It has a simple Fair Isle pattern worked over the body with a border The round neckline fits neatly and the tops of the sleeves are full and gathered in at the shoulders.

Sizes

To fit 86cm/34in bust loosely
Length to shoulder, 54cm/21¼in
Sleeve seam, 41cm/16¼in

You will need

5 × 50g balls of Scheepjeswol
 Voluma (85% acrylic, 15% kid
 mohair) in main colour A
1 ball of same in contrast colour B
1 ball of same in contrast colour C
One pair 3¼mm/No 10 needles
One pair 4mm/No 8 needles
One 3¼mm/No 10 circular needle,
 80cm/30in long
One 4mm/No 8 circular needle,
 80cm/30in long
Eight buttons

Tension

22 sts and 26 rows to 10cm/4in over patt worked on 4mm/No 8 needles

Note

Strand yarn not in use across back of work. When more than 5 sts are worked in any colour, weave in yarn not in use across back of work.

Jacket body

With 3¼mm/No 10 circular needle and A cast of 215 sts and work in one piece to underarm.
1st row K1, *P1, K1, rep from * to end.
2nd row P1, *K1, P1, rep from * to end.
Rep these 2 rows once more.
5th row (buttonhole row) Rib 2 sts, cast off 2 sts, rib to end.
6th row Rib to end, casting on 2 sts above those cast off in previous row.
Work 3 more rows in rib.
Next row (inc row) Rib 7 sts and sl these on to a saftey pin and leave for front band, change to 4mm/No 8 circular needle, P6, (inc in next st, P8) 21 times, inc in next st, P5, turn

and leave rem 7 sts on safety pin for other front band. 223 sts.
Beg with a K row cont in st st and work the first 7 rows of patt from chart 1, then P one row with A.
**Next row K3 A, *1 B, 3 A, rep from * to end.
Beg with a P row, work 3 rows st st in A.
Next row K1 A, *1 B, 3 A, rep from * to last 2 sts, 1 B, 1 A.
Beg with a P row work 3 rows st st in A.**
Rep last 8 rows until work measures about 29cm/11½in from beg, ending with 3 rows st st in A.
Beg with a K row work 8 rows of patt from chart 2.

Divide for armholes

Next row Using B, K52 sts, cast off 8 sts for armhole, K103 sts for back cast off 8 sts for other armhole, K52 sts.
Cont on last set of 52 sts for left front and P one row in A.

Chart 1

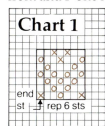

end st ⌐↑ rep 6 sts

Chart 2

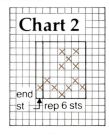

end st ⌐↑ rep 6 sts

Beg with a K row work 2 rows in patt from chart 3.

Shape armhole

Keeping patt correct throughout as shown on chart 3, cast off at beg of next and every alt row 2 sts twice and one st twice. 46 sts.
Cont in patt from chart 3 until 41 rows have been worked, ending with a K row.

Shape neck

Keeping patt correct throughout as shown on chart 3, cast off at beg of next and every alt row 10 sts once, 4 sts once, 2 sts once and one st once, ending with a P row.

Shape shoulder

Cast off at beg of next and foll alt row 14 sts once and 15 sts once.
With Ws of work facing rejoin A to 103 sts for back and P one row.
Beg with a K row work 2 rows in patt from chart 3.

Shape armholes

Keeping patt correct throughout as shown on chart 3, cast off at beg of next and every row 2 sts 4 times and one st 4 times. 91 sts.
Cont in patt from chart 3 until 43 rows have been worked, ending with a K row.

Chart 3

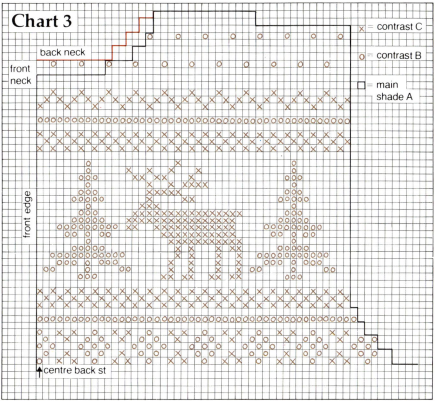

x = contrast C

o = contrast B

□ = main shade A

Shape neck

Next row Keeping patt correct throughout P35 sts, cast off 21 sts for centre back neck, P35 sts. Complete right shoulder first. K one row. Cast off 2 sts at beg of next and foll alt row, ending with a P row.

Shape shoulder

Cast off at beg of next and every row 14 sts for shoulder, 2 sts for neck and 15 sts for shoulder. With Rs of work facing rejoin yarn to rem 35 sts and complete to match right shoulder, reversing shapings. With Ws of work facing rejoin A to rem 52 sts for right front. Complete to match left front, reversing all shapings.

Sleeves

With 3¼mm/No 10 needles and A cast on 43 sts. Work 4cm/1½in rib as given for body, ending with a 1st row.
Next row (inc row) P2, *inc in next st, P1, rep from * to last st, P1. 63 sts.
Change to 4mm/No 8 needles. Beg with a K row cont in st st and work first 7 rows of patt from chart 1, then P one row with A.
Cont in patt as given for body from ** to **, inc one st at each end of next and every foll 6th row until there are 83 sts, then cont without shaping until sleeve measures 37cm/14½in from beg, ending with 3 rows in A.

Shape top

Beg with a K row, cont in patt as given on chart 4, shaping top as shown on chart.

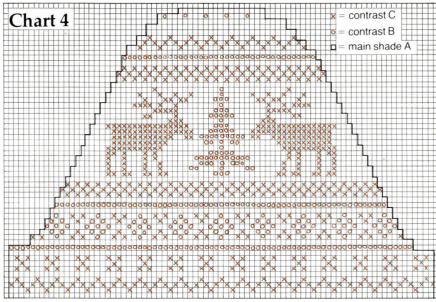

Chart 4

× = contrast C
○ = contrast B
□ = main shade A

Button band

With Rs of work facing and 3¼mm/No 10 needles rejoin A to 7 sts on safety pin on left front edge, inc in first st, rib to end. 8 sts.
Cont in rib until band, when slightly stretched, fits along front edge to neck edge, ending with a Ws row. Leave sts on holder. Tack band in place.
Mark positions for 8 buttons, first to come on 5th row of welt and last to come in neckband, 5 rows above sts on holder, with 6 more evenly spaced between.

Buttonhole band

With Ws of work facing and 3¼mm/No 10 needles rejoin A to 7 sts on safety pin on right front edge, inc in first st, rib to end.
Work as given for button band,

making buttonholes as markers are reached as before. Do not cut yarn.

Neckband

Join shoulder seams.
With Rs of work facing, 3¼mm/No 10 needles and A rib across 8 sts of right front band, pick up and K24 sts up right front neck and 8 sts down right back neck, K across back neck sts on holder, pick up and K8 sts up left back neck and 24 sts down left front neck, then rib across rem 8 sts of left front band. 101 sts.
Cont in rib for 4cm/1½in, making buttonhole as before on 4th row. Cast off in rib.

To make up

Do not press. Join sleeve seams. Set in sleeves. Sew on button and buttonhole bands. Sew on buttons.

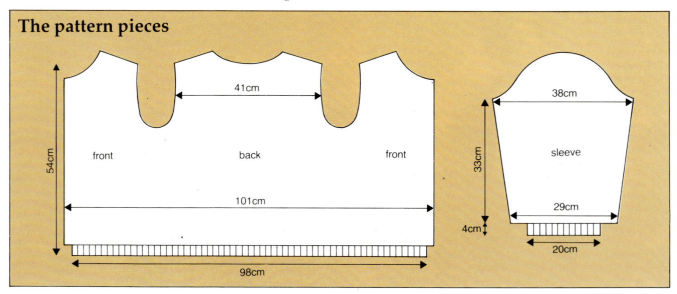

The pattern pieces

front   back   front

41cm
54cm
101cm
98cm

sleeve
38cm
33cm
29cm
4cm
20cm

Norwegian-style jersey

The crew-necked jersey features the traditional dropped shoulder line of a Norwegian design.

A small seeding design is used as an all-over pattern on the body and sleeves. At the yoke level and the top of the sleeves a geometric border is worked and the garment is completed with a broad band of snowflake motifs.

Sizes

To fit 86–91cm/34–36in bust
Length to shoulder, 61cm/24in
Sleeve seam, 49cm/19¼in

You will need

8×50g balls of Scheepjeswol Luzern (55% wool, 45% acrylic) in main colour A
4 balls of same in contrast colour B
One pair 4mm/No 8 needles
One pair 5mm/No 6 needles
Set of four 4mm/No 8 needles pointed at both ends

Tension

20 sts and 24 rows to 10cm/4in over patt worked on 5mm/No 6 needles

Back

With 4mm/No 8 needles and B cast on 101 sts.
1st row (Rs) K1, *P1, K1, rep from * to end.
2nd row P1, *K1, P1, rep from * to end.
Rep these 2 rows for 5cm/2in, ending with a 2nd row. Change to 5mm/No 6 needles. Commence border and seeding patt.
1st row (Rs) With B, K to end.
2nd row With B, P to end. Join in A.
3rd row K1 A, *K3 B, K1 A, rep from * to end.
4th row P2 A, *P1 B, P3 A, rep from * to last 3 sts, P1 B, P2 A.
5th row With A, inc in first st, K to last 2 sts, inc in next st, K1. 103 sts.
6th row With A, P to end.
7th row K1 B, *K5 A, K1 B, rep from * to end.
8th row With A, P to end.
9th row With A, K to end.
10th row P3 A, *P1 B, P5 A, rep from * to last 4 sts, P1 B, P3 A.
11th row With A, K to end.
Rep the 6th to 11th rows until work

measures 39cm/15¼in from beg, ending with a Ws row.

Shape armholes

Keeping patt correct as set, cast off 7 sts at beg of next 2 rows. 89 sts. Cont without shaping until work measures about 41cm/16¼in from beg, ending with a 6th patt row. Beg with a K row cont in st st, working yoke patt from chart to end. Cast off with B.

Front

Work as given for back, shaping neck as shown on chart.

Sleeves

With 4mm/No 8 needles and B cast on 37 sts. Work 5cm/2in K1, P1 rib as given for back, ending with a 1st row.
Next row (inc row) Rib 3 sts, *K1, P twice into next st, rep from * to last 2 sts, rib 2. 53 sts.
Change to 5mm/No 6 needles.

Work in border and seeding patt as given for back, inc one st at each end of 5th row as given and every foll 4th row, working extra sts into patt, until there are 89 sts and work measures about 37cm/14½in, ending with a 6th patt row. Beg with a K row cont in st st without shaping, working in patt from chart until 30 rows have been completed, then work first 3 rows of chart again. Cast off loosely with B.

Neckband

Join shoulder seams. With Rs of work facing, set of four 4mm/No 8 needles and B, pick up and K33 sts across back neck, 22 sts down left front neck, 11 sts across front neck and 22 sts up right front neck. 88 sts. Cont in rounds of K1, P1 rib for 8cm/3¼in. Cast off loosely in rib with B.

To make up

Do not press. Sew in sleeves, setting in last 8 rows to cast off sts at armholes. Join side and sleeve seams. Fold neckband in half to Ws and sl st down.

Left: A typical Scandinavian design.

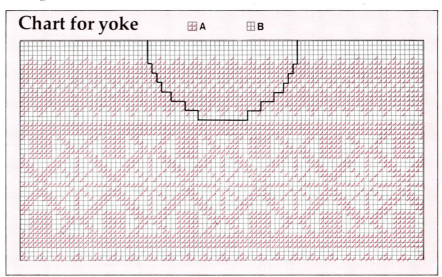

Chart for yoke ▦ A ▦ B

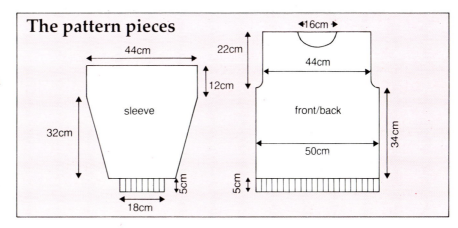

The pattern pieces

sleeve — 44cm, 32cm, 18cm, 5cm

front/back — 16cm, 22cm, 44cm, 12cm, 34cm, 50cm, 5cm

Alternative motifs for Scandinavian knitting

Traditional Scandinavian designs are lively using boldly contrasting colours. Modern versions use a range of colours including the pastel shades.

Stag designs vary from magnificent reindeer with full antlers to gentle does and fawns.

Snowflake designs can be worked as a single motif or all-over patterns.

Peasant figures can be used one or two at a time as a motif, or linking hands as a border, similar to a string of paper dolls.

Geometric designs are used one above the other in bands as all-over

fabrics or as borders separating one type of motif from another. They are not suitable as single motifs.

Pine tree designs vary from simplistic outlines to full Christmas tree shapes.

Seeding patterns are used specifically as regular all-over patterns, parti-

Stag design

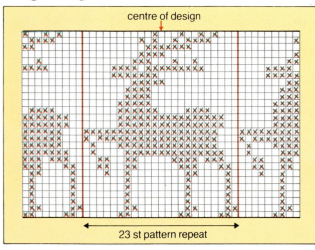

23 st pattern repeat

With A cast on multiples of 23 sts plus two, eg 48, or position 25 sts as a single motif.
1st row (Rs) K1 A, *K1 A, join in B, K2 B, K4 A, K2 B, K7 A, K2 B, K5 A, rep from * to last st, K1 A.
Beg with a P row and 2nd row of chart, cont in patt until 27 rows have been completed.

Snowflake design

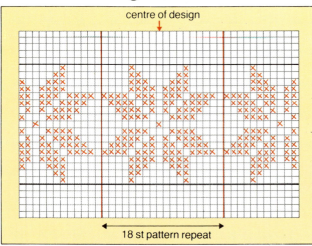

18 st pattern repeat

With A cast on multiples of 18 sts plus one, eg 37, or position 19 sts as a single motif.
1st row (Rs) *K5 A, join in B, K1 B, K7 A, K1 B, K4 A, rep from * to last st, K1 A.
Beg with a P row and 2nd row of chart, cont in patt until 18 rows have been completed.

Peasant figures

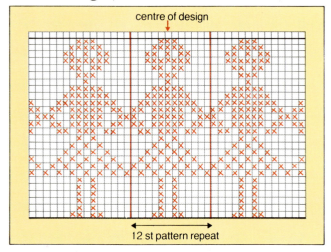

12 st pattern repeat

With A cast on multiples of 12 sts plus one, eg 25, or position 13 sts as a single motif.
1st row (Rs) *K4 A, join in B, K2 B, K1 A, K2 B, K3 A, rep from * to last st, K1 A.
Beg with a P row and 2nd row of chart, cont in patt until 26 rows have been completed.

Geometric design

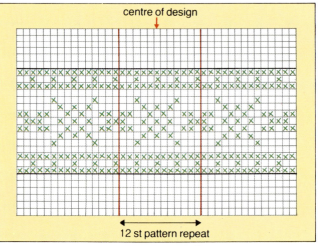

12 st pattern repeat

With B cast multiples of 12 sts plus one, eg 25.
1st row (Rs) With B, K to end.
2nd row With B, P1, join in A, *P2A, P1B, rep from * to end.
3rd row With B, K to end. Beg with a P row and 4th row of chart, cont in patt until 16 rows are completed.

cularly at points where shaping is required.

The designs given below can be substituted for the ones given on the cardigan on pages 87-9 or the jersey on pages 90-91. Use the charts given on pages 87, 88 and 91 to work out how many repeats of your substitute pattern will fit and the best position for them. Or you could try combining motifs – the snowflake and the pine tree for example.

The method for positioning a motif accurately is given in the Professional Touch below, using the reindeer as an example. You could, of course, choose your own motif to use instead of any of those given here.

Traditionally only two colours are used on a stocking stitch fabric. The yarn is stranded or woven across the back when not in use. Take care not to pull it tight when working or the fabric will not lie flat.

Pine tree design

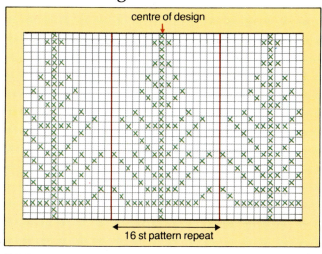

centre of design

←— 16 st pattern repeat —→

With A cast on multiples of 16 sts plus one, eg 33, or position 17 sts as a single motif.
1st row (Rs) *K8 A, join in B, K1 B, K7 A, rep from * to last st, K1 A.
Beg with a P row and 2nd row of chart, cont in patt until 27 rows have been completed.

Seeding pattern

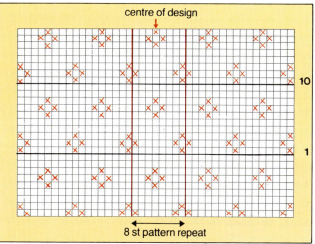

centre of design

10

1

←— 8 st pattern repeat —→

With A cast on multiples of 8 sts plus one, eg 25.
1st row (Rs) Join in B, *K1 B, K7 A, rep from * to last st, K1 B.
Beg with a P row and 2nd row of chart, cont in patt until 10 rows have been completed. Repeat these 10 rows for an all-over pattern.

PROFESSIONAL TOUCH

Positioning a motif accurately

Determine the exact centre of the motif you wish to use and the centre of the background fabric. Check that sufficient rows remain to complete the motif and that it is positioned clear of any shaping.

For example, you can feature the stag motif in this chapter on either side of the yoke and head of the sleeves of the jersey, instead of the band of snowflakes. (You cannot work this as a central motif as the front neck shaping will interfere.) Complete the armhole shaping on the body. The centre stitch on the motif is the 12th, as marked.

Working from chart

Work the first four rows from the jersey chart and begin the stag on the 5th row. The centre stitch of the body is the 45th stitch so a stag is positioned, to the nearest stitch, centrally on the 44 stitches on either side of the yoke, as follows:

5th row (Rs) K10 A, K2 B, K4 A, K2 B, K7 A, K2 B, K17 A, K1 A for centre st, now work back across the chart from the 44th st from left to right to reverse the position of the stag on the other side of the yoke.

6th row Beg at the right-hand edge of the stag chart, P9 A, P2 B, P4 A, P2 B, P7 A, P2 B, P18 A, P1 A for centre st, now work back across the chart from the 44th st from left to right to reverse the position.

Continue working the 27 rows of the stag in this way, then purl

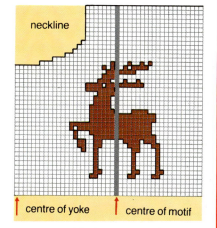

neckline

↑ centre of yoke   ↑ centre of motif

one row with A.
Work from the 31st row of the jersey chart to complete the yoke, noting that 2 extra rows have been worked.
Work the head of the sleeves in the same way, noting that 2 extra rows have been worked.

Cricket-style pullover with cable panels

Knit this cabled pullover in a choice of sizes suitable for men or women. The yarn comes in a wide range of colours to suit all ages and tastes.

Sizes

To fit 86 [91:96:101]cm/ 34 [36:38:40]in bust/chest
Length to shoulder, 62.5 [65:67.5:70]cm/25 [25½:26½:27½]in
The figures in [] refer to the 91/36, 96/38 and 101cm/40in sizes respectively

You will need

8 [9:9:10]×40g balls Sirdar Wash 'n' Wear Double Crêpe (55% Bri-Nylon, 45% acrylic)
One pair 3¼mm/No 10 needles
Set of four 3¼mm/No 10 needles
One pair 4mm/No 8 needles
Cable needle

Tension

24 sts and 32 rows to 10cm/4in over st st worked on 4mm/No 8 needles

Back

With 3¼mm/No 10 needles cast on 122 [130:138:146] sts.
1st row (Rs) K2, *P2, K2, rep from * to end.
2nd row P2, *K2, P2, rep from * to end.
Rep these 2 rows for 7cm/2¾in, ending with a 1st row.
Next row (inc row) Rib 1 [2:6:1] sts, *inc in next st, rib 9 [8:8:8], rep from * to last 1 [2:6:1] sts, rib to end. 134 [144:152:162] sts.
Change to 4mm/No 8 needles.
Commence patt.
1st row (Rs) K13 [6:10:15], *P3, K6, P3, K12, rep from * 3 [4:4:4] more times, P3, K6, P3, K13 [6:10:15].
2nd row P13 [6:10:15], *K3, P6, K3, P12, rep from * 3 [4:4:4] more times, K3, P6, K3, P13 [6:10:15].
3rd row K13 [6:10:15], *P3, sl next 3 sts on to cable needle and hold at front of work, K the next 3 sts, K3 from cable needle – **called C6F**, P3, K12, rep from * 3 [4:4:4] more times, P3, C6F, P3, K13 [6:10:15].
4th row As 2nd.

Left: Cable panels, alternated with panels of stocking stitch, give these pullovers their traditional look.

Rep 1st and 2nd rows 3 more times. These 10 rows form pattern. Cont in patt until back measures 37.5 [39:40.5:42]cm/14¾ [15¼:16:16½]in from beg, ending with a Ws row.

Shape armholes

Keeping the patt correct, cast off at the beg of next and every foll row 4 sts twice and 3 sts twice.
Dec one st each end of next 3 rows, then dec one st each end of every foll alt row 4 [6:8:10] times. 106 [112:116:122] sts.
Cont in patt without shaping until armhole measures 25 [26:27:28]cm/ 9¾ [10¼:10¾:11]in from beg, ending with a Ws row.

Shape shoulders

Cast off at beg of next and every foll row 14 [15:16:17] sts 4 times and 50 [52:52:54] sts once.

Front

Work as given for back to start of armhole shaping, ending with a Ws row.

Shape armholes and neck

**Next row Cast off 4 sts, patt across 63 [68:72:77] sts (incl st on right-hand needle), turn leaving rem sts on holder. Complete left shoulder first.
Next row Work 2 tog, patt to end. Keeping patt correct, cast off 3 sts at beg of next row. Dec one st at armhole edge on foll 3 rows, then dec one st at armhole edge on every foll alt row 4 [6:8:10] times, *at the same time* dec one st at neck edge every alt row until 28 [30:32:34] sts rem.

Cont without shaping until armhole measures same as back to shoulder, ending at armhole edge.

Shape shoulder

Cast off 14 [15:16:17] sts at beg of next and foll alt row.******
With Rs facing, rejoin yarn to rem sts and patt to end of row.
Complete right shoulder to match left shoulder working from ** to ** reversing all shaping.

Armbands

Join shoulder seams.
With Rs facing and 3¼mm/No 10 needles pick up and K150 [158:162:170] sts round armhole.
Work 3cm/1¼in K2, P2 rib as given for back.
Cast off loosely in rib.

Neckband

With Rs facing and set of four 3¼mm/No 10 needles pick up and K48 [48:52:54] sts from back neck, 76 [80:84:88] sts down left front neck, one st from centre of V (mark this st with a thread) and 74 [78:82:84] sts up right front neck. 199 [207:219:227] sts.
1st round *P2, K2, rep from * to within 4 sts of marked st, P2, K2 tog, K1, K2 tog tbl, **P2, K2, rep from ** to end of round.
Cont working in rib as set, dec one st on each side of marked st on every round until neckband measures 3cm/1¼in.
Cast off loosely in rib.

To make up

Do not press. Join side seams.

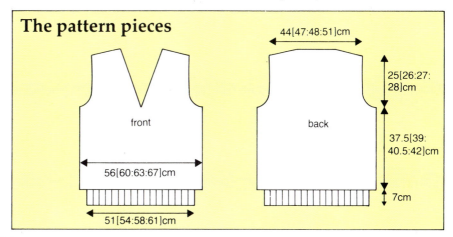

The pattern pieces

front

56[60:63:67]cm

51[54:58:61]cm

44[47:48:51]cm

back

25[26:27:28]cm

37.5[39:40.5:42]cm

7cm

A new look for the traditional Argyle

This stylish waistcoat in Argyle pattern sounds two new fashion notes: it is knitted in pastel shades and a cotton yarn, cool and crisp worn with light-weight trousers and an open-necked shirt.

If you prefer to have only one contrast colour, you can use the main colour within the pattern, too.

Sizes

To fit 91 [97:102]cm/36 [38:40]in chest
Length to shoulder, 59 [62:65]cm/ 23¼ [24½:25½]in
The figures in [] refer to 97/38 and 102cm/40in sizes respectively

You will need

3 [4:4]×50g balls of Pingouin Corrida No 3, (60% cotton, 40% acrylic) in colour A
1×50g ball each of contrasts B and C
One pair 2¾mm/No 12 needles
One pair 3mm/No 11 needles
Five buttons

Tension

28 sts and 37 rows to 10cm/4in over st st worked on 3mm/No 11 needles

Note

For the Argyle pattern on the fronts work from the chart using a separate small ball for each block of colour.

Twist the yarns round each other when changing colour during a row.

Back

With 2¾mm/No 12 needles and A cast on 126 [132:138] sts. Work in K1, P1 rib for 6cm/2¼in ending with Rs row.
Next row (inc row) Rib 6 [12:18], (inc in next st, rib 14) 8 times. 134 [140:146] sts.
Change to 3mm/No 11 needles. Beg with a K row work in st st until back measures 37 [39:41]cm/14½ [15¼: 16¼]in from beg, ending on a P row.

Shape armholes

Cast off at the beg of next and every following row 5 sts twice, 2 sts 8 times, and one st 4 [6:8] times. 104 [108:112] sts. Cont without shaping until armholes measure 22 [23:24]cm/8¾ [9:9½]in from beg, ending with a P row.

Shape shoulders and neck

Cast off 8 sts at beg of next 4 rows.
Next row Cast off 8 sts, K10 [11:12] sts and leave these for right shoulder, cast off next 36 [38:40] sts for centre back neck, K18 [19:20] sts. Complete left shoulder first.
Cast off at beg of next and every row 8 sts once, 4 sts once and 6 [7:8] sts once.

With Ws of work facing rejoin yarn to neck edge of right shoulder. Cast off at beg of next 2 rows 4 sts once and 6 [7:8] sts once.

Right front

With 2¾mm/No 12 needles and A cast on 64 [66:68] sts. Work in K1, P1 rib for 6cm/2¼in ending with Rs row.
Next row (inc row) Rib 20 [16:10], (inc in next st, rib 10) 3 [4:5] times, rib 11 [6:3]. 67 [70:73] sts.
Change to 3mm/No 11 needles. Beg with a K row cont in st st, working the Argyle patt from the chart and joining in colours as required.
1st row K1 B, (23 C, 1 B) 2 [2:3] times, then 18 [21:0] C.
Cont in patt as now set until work measures 37 [39:41] cm/14½ [15¼: 16¼]in from beg, ending with a P row.

Shape front and armhole

Dec one st at beg of next (front edge) and every alt row 6 [7:8] times, then every 4th row 16 times, *at the same time* cast off at beg of every Ws row (armhole edge) 5 sts once, 2 sts 4 times and one st 2 [3:4] times. 30 [31:32] sts.
Cont in patt without shaping until work measures same as for back to shoulder ending at armhole edge.

Shape shoulder

Cast off at beg of next and every alt row 8 sts 3 times and 6 [7:8] sts once.

Left front

Work as given for right front, reversing the patt from the chart and all shapings.

Left front border

With 2¾mm/No 12 needles and A cast on 172 [182:192] sts. Work in K1, P1 rib for 4 rows.
Next row (buttonhole row) Rib to last 95 [102:109] sts, cast off 2 sts, *rib 20 [22:24], cast off 2 sts, rep from * 3 more times, rib to end.
Next row Rib to end casting on 2 sts above those cast off in previous row.
Work 4 more rows in rib. Cast off loosely in rib.

Right front and back neck border

With 2¾mm/No 12 needles and A cast on 218 [230:242] sts. Work in K1, P1 rib for 10 rows. Cast off in rib.

Chart for Argyle pattern

☐ = colour B   ☐ = colour C

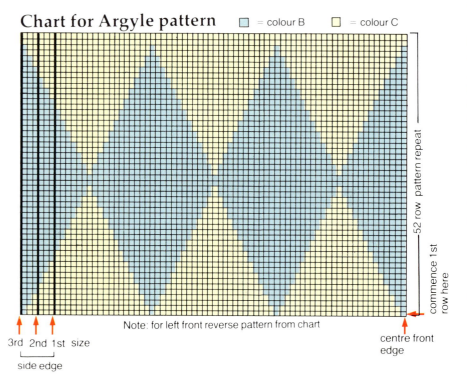

Note: for left front reverse pattern from chart

52 row pattern repeat

commence 1st row here

centre front edge

3rd 2nd 1st size

side edge

Above: A modern interpretation of a traditional pattern in pastel colours. The true Argyle patterns are knitted in grey or beige, with red and yellow diamonds and a dark green criss-cross.

Armhole borders

With 2¾mm needles and A cast on 150 [156:162] sts. Work in K1, P1 rib for 10 rows. Cast off loosely in rib.

Making up

Do not press the pieces as this will spoil the yarn. Join right shoulder seam. Sew on borders with the ends meeting at left shoulder. Join left shoulder seam and ends of borders. Sew on armhole borders easing them slightly around the curves. Join side seams and ends of borders. Sew on buttons.

The pattern pieces

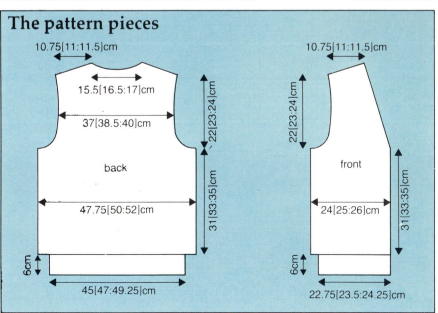

back

10.75[11:11.5]cm
15.5[16.5:17]cm
37[38.5:40]cm
47.75[50:52]cm
22[23:24]cm
31[33:35]cm
6cm
45[47:49.25]cm

front

10.75[11:11.5]cm
22[23:24]cm
24[25:26]cm
31[33:35]cm
6cm
22.75[23.5:24.25]cm

Man's geometric patterned jersey

The back and front of this chunky jersey are worked in a geometric pattern. This is repeated on elbow patches which strengthen and decorate the plain sleeves. The welt and cuffs are knitted in rib and the roll neck collar in plain stocking stitch.

Sizes

To fit 97–102 [107–112]cm/38–40 [42–44]in chest
Length to shoulder, 69 [71]cm/ 27 [28]in
Sleeve seam, 51 [53]cm/20 [21]in
The figures in [] refer to the 107–112cm/42–44in size only

You will need

6 [7]×50g balls of Robin Reward Double Double (60% Courtelle, 40% Bri-nylon) in main colour A
2 [3] balls of same in contrast colour B
2 [3] balls of same in contrast colour C
2 [3]×50g balls of Robin Landscape Chunky (75% acrylic, 25% wool) in contrast colour D
2 [2]×50g balls of Robin Softspun (52% wool, 47% acrylic, 1% nylon) in contrast colour E
2 [3]×50g balls *each* of Robin Reward Double Knitting and Robin Reward 4 ply (60% Courtelle, 40% Bri-nylon) used together as contrast colour F
One pair 5mm/No 6 needles
One pair 5½mm/No 5 needles
One 5mm/No 6 circular needle 60cm/24in long
Dolly bobbin or French knitting kit

Tension

14 sts and 19 rows to 10cm/4in over st st worked on 5½mm/No 5 needles

Back

With 5mm/No 6 needles and A cast on 80 [86] sts. Work 7 [9]cm/3 [3½]in K1, P1 rib, ending with a Rs row.
Next row (inc row) Rib 5 [8] sts, *pick up loop lying between sts and K tbl – **called M1**, rib 10 sts, rep from * to last 5 [8] sts, M1, rib to end. 88 [94] sts.
Change to 5½mm/No 5 needles. Commence patt noting that separate balls of yarn are used for each colour and that yarns are twisted at back of work when changing colours to avoid a hole. **
1st row of chart (Rs) K24 [27] A, K22 D, K3 E, K39 [42] C.
2nd row of chart K39 [42] C, P4 E, P21 D, P24 [27] A.
3rd row of chart K24 [27] A, K20 D, K5 E, K39 [42] C.
4th row of chart K39 [42] C, P6 E, P19 D, P24 [27] A.
Cont working in patt from the chart in this way, working section in C in g st and remainder in st st, until 30 rows have been completed. Cont in patt from chart working across all sts in st st until 98 [100] rows have been completed.

Shape neck

Next row Patt 32 [35] sts from chart, turn and leave rem sts on holder. Complete right shoulder first.
Patt one row, then dec one st at neck edge on next and every foll alt row until 28 [31] sts rem.
Cont without shaping until all rows of chart have been completed. Cast off.

Right: There are many possible combinations of colours for this attractive jersey to give your own original look to this designer garment.

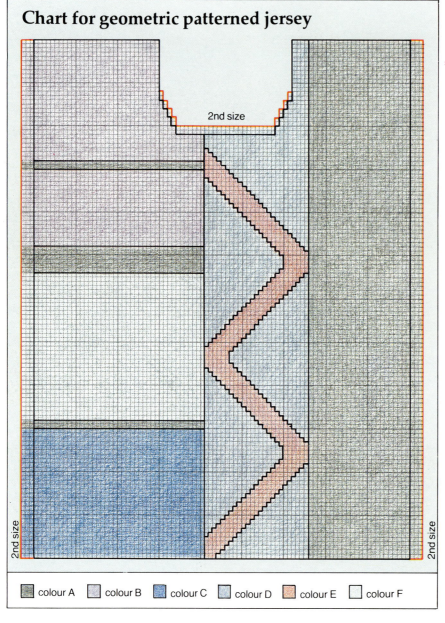

Chart for geometric patterned jersey

2nd size

2nd size

2nd size

| colour A | colour B | colour C | colour D | colour E | colour F |

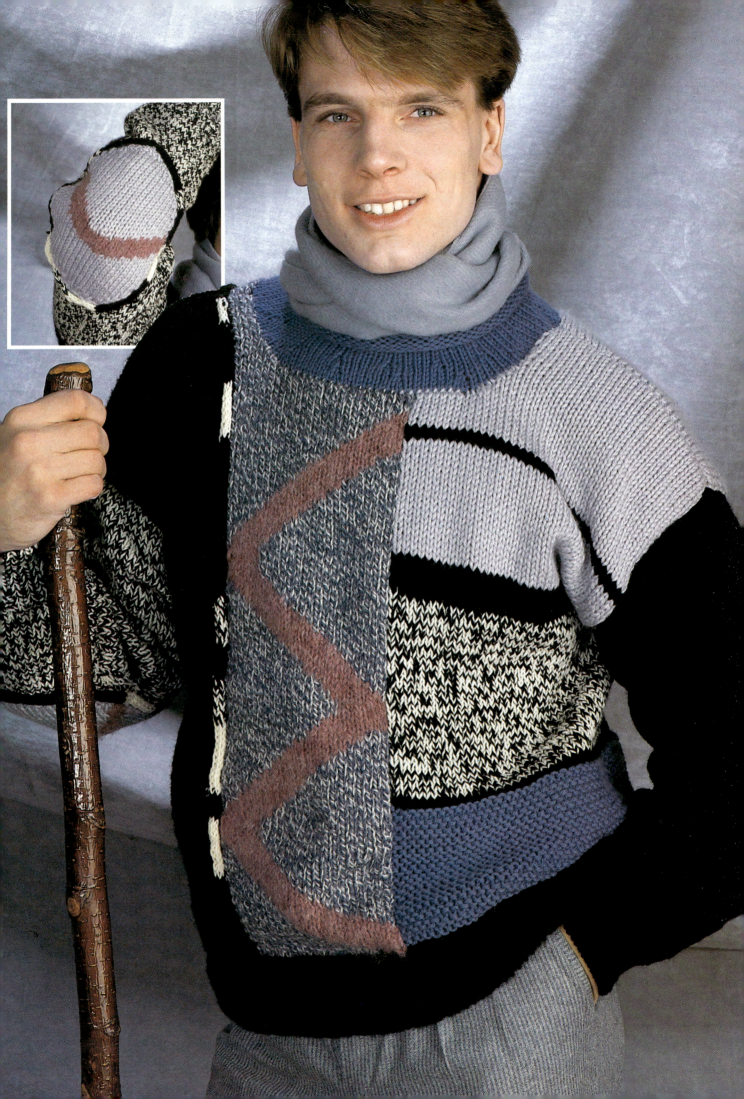

Chart for elbow patches

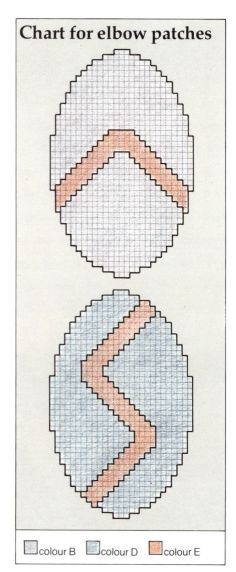

☐ colour B ☐ colour D ☐ colour E

With Rs of work facing leave first 24 sts on holder for centre back neck, join in appropriate yarn to rem sts and patt to end. Complete to match first side reversing shaping.

Front

Work as given for back to **.
Reading Ws rows from right to left and Rs rows from left to right to reverse the patt, commence patt.
1st row of chart K39 [42] C, K3 E, K22 D, K24 [27] A.
2nd row of chart P24 [27] A, P21 D, P4 E, K39 [42] C.
3rd row of chart K39 [42] C, K5 E, K20 D, K24 [27] A.
4th row of chart P24 [27] A, P19 D, P6 E, K39 [42] C.
Complete as given for back.

Right sleeve

With 5mm/No 6 needles and E cast

on 44 [48] sts. Work 7cm/3in K1, P1 rib.
Next row (inc row) Rib 4 [3] sts, *M1, rib 7 [6] sts, rep from * to last 5 [3] sts, M1, rib to end. 50 [56] sts. Change to 5½mm/No 5 needles. Beg with a K row cont in st st, inc one st at each end of every foll 5th row until there are 78 [84] sts. Cont without shaping until sleeve measures 51 [53]cm/20 [21]in from beg, ending with a P row. Cast off.

Left sleeve

Using A instead of E, work as given for right sleeve.

Collar

Join shoulder seams.
With Rs of work facing and 5mm/No 6 circular needle and C, beg at left shoulder seam, pick up and K15 sts down left front neck, K across 24 sts on holder, pick up and K15 sts up right front neck and 15 sts down right back neck, K across 24 sts on holder and pick up and K15 sts up left back neck. 108 sts.
Mark beg of round with contrast thread.
K two rounds.
Next round (dec round) *K7, K2 tog, rep from * to end.
K two rounds.
Next round (dec round) *K6, K2 tog, rep from * to end.
K four rounds.
Next round (dec round) *K5, K2 tog, rep from * to end. 72 sts.
K ten rounds. Cast off.

Right elbow patch

With 5½mm/No 5 needles and B

cast on 3 sts.
Beg with a K row cont in st st working in patt from chart and inc as foll:
1st row (Rs) K into front, back and front of first st, K1, K into front, back and front of last st.
2nd row P into front, back and front of first st, P to last st, P into front, back and front of last st.
3rd row K twice into first st, K to last st, K twice into last st.
4th row P twice into first st, P to last st, P twice into last st.
Cont in patt from chart in this way, inc one st at each end of next and foll 3 alt rows, then on foll 4th row. Work 8 rows without shaping, then dec one st at each end of next and foll 4th row, then on foll 3 alt rows and next 3 rows.
Next row K3 tog, K to last 3 sts, K3 tog.
Next row P3 tog, P1, P3 tog.
Cast off rem 3 sts.

Left elbow patch

Use chart for left elbow patch and complete as for right elbow patch.

Rouleau

With dolly bobbin or French knitting kit and A and F, make two lengths of rouleau to go round elbow patches and one for front and back, beg and ending at top of rib.

To make up

Do not press. Sew on elbow patches. Sew rouleau around patches and along front and back between A and D sections. Sew in sleeves. Join seams. Allow collar to roll back.

The pattern pieces

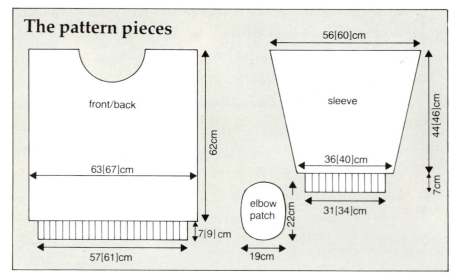

Raglan-sleeve jersey with pouch pocket

This classic crew-neck jersey in stocking stitch, is quick and easy to knit. The pouch pocket is ideal for keeping hands warm on cold winter days and adds an attractive feature to an otherwise plain garment. All the ribbing is knitted in a contrast colour.

Sizes

To fit 81 [86:91:97:102:107]cm/ 32 [34:36:38:40:42]in bust/chest
Length to centre back neck, 56 [57:58:59:60:61]cm/ 22 [22½:22¾:23¼:23½:24]in
Sleeve seam, 43 [44:45:46:47:48]cm/ 17 [17¼:17¾:18:18½:19]in
The figures in [] refer to the 86/34, 91/36, 97/38, 102/40 and 107cm/42in sizes respectively

You will need

6 [7:7:8:8:9]×50g balls of Hayfield Grampian Double Knitting (45% acrylic, 40% Bri-nylon, 15% wool) in main colour A
1 [1:1:1:2:2] balls of same in contrast colour B
One pair 3¼mm/No 10 needles
One pair 4mm/No 8 needles
Set of four 3¼mm/No 10 needles pointed at both ends

Tension

22 sts and 30 rows to 10cm/4in over st st worked on 4mm/No 8 needles

Back

With 3¼mm/No 10 needles and B cast on 99 [105:111:117:123:129] sts.
1st row (Rs) K1, *P1, K1, rep from * to end.
2nd row P1, *K1, P1, rep from * to end.
Rep these 2 rows for 5cm/2in, ending with a 2nd row. Break off B. **
Change to 4mm/No 8 needles. Join in A. Beg with a K row cont in st st until work measures 36cm/14¼in from beg, ending with a P row.

Shape raglan armholes

Cast off 5 sts at beg of next 2 rows.
Next row K1, sl 1, K1, psso, K to last 3 sts, K2 tog, K1.
Next row P to end.

Right: Use a plain or tweedy yarn as the main fabric and a toning colour for the ribbing on this stylish jersey.

Above: detail of pocket edgings.

Rep last 2 rows until
31 [33:35:37:39:41] sts rem, ending
with a P row.
Leave sts on holder for centre back
neck.

Front

With 4mm/No 8 needles and A cast
on 55 [55:57:57:59:59] sts for pocket
lining. Beg with a K row work 10
rows st st. Leave sts on holder.
Work front as given for back to **.
Change to 4mm/No 8 needles. Join
in A. Beg with a K row work 10
rows st st.

Place pocket

Next row K22 [25:27:30:32:35] sts, sl
next 55 [55:57:57:59:59] sts on to a
thread and leave for time being, K
across pocket lining sts, K to end.
Beg with a P row cont in st st for
13 [13:14:14:15:15]cm/
5 [5:5½:5½:6:6]in, ending with a
P row. Leave sts for time being.
Do not break off yarn.

Complete pocket front

With Rs of work facing and 4mm/
No 8 needles, join in another ball of
yarn to sts on thread and work to
match length of first piece, ending
with a P row.
Break off yarn. Leave sts on needle.

Join pocket front and lining

Next row With Rs facing return to
where yarn was left,
K22 [25:27:30:32:35] sts, place sts of
pocket front in front of work and K
tog one st from each needle until all
sts are worked, then K rem
22 [25:27:30:32:35] sts.
Cont as given for back until
49 [51:53:55:57:59] sts rem in raglan
armhole shaping, ending with a P
row.

Shape neck

Next row K1, sl 1, K1, psso, K14 sts,

turn and leave rem sts on spare
needle.
Next row P to end.
Next row K1, sl 1, K1, psso, K to last
3 sts, sl 1, K1, psso, K1.
Rep last 2 rows 5 times more, then
dec at armhole edge only on foll 2
alt rows.
Cast off rem 2 sts.
With Rs of work facing, sl first
15 [17:19:21:23:25] sts on to holder,
rejoin yarn to rem sts, K to last 3 sts,
K2 tog, K1.
Next row P to end.
Next row K1, K2 tog, K to last 3 sts,
K2 tog, K1.
Complete to match first side.

Sleeves

With 3¼mm/No 10 needles and B
cast on 41 [43:45:47:49:51] sts. Work
5cm/2in rib as given for back,
ending with a 1st row.
Next row (inc row) Rib
5 [6:5:6:3:4] sts, *pick up loop lying
between needles and K tbl – **called
M1**, rib 10 [10:7:7:6:6] sts, rep from
* to last 6 [7:5:6:4:5] sts, M1, rib to
end. 45 [47:51:53:57:59] sts.
Break off B. Join in A. Change to
4mm/No 8 needles. Beg with a K
row cont in st st inc one st at each
end of 5th and every foll 8th row
until there are 71 [75:79:83:87:91] sts.
Cont without shaping until sleeve
measures 43 [44:45:46:47:48]cm/
17 [17¼:17¾:18:18½:19]in from
beg, ending with a P row. Place a
marker at each end of last row then
work a further 6 rows.

Shape top

Next row K1, sl 1, K1, psso, K to last

3 sts, K2 tog, K1.
Next row P to end.
Rep last 2 rows until 13 sts rem,
ending with a P row. Leave sts on
holder.

Neckband

Join raglan seams, sewing the last 6
rows of sleeves from markers to cast
off sts at armholes.
With Rs of work facing, set of four
3¼mm/No 10 needles and B, K
across sts of back neck and left
sleeve K2 tog at seam, pick up and
K10 sts down left front neck, K
across front neck sts, pick up and
K10 sts up right front neck, then K
across sts of right sleeve K last st of
sleeve tog with first st of back neck.
90 [94:98:102:106:110] sts.
Cont in rounds of K1, P1 rib for
5cm/2in. Cast off loosely in rib.

Pocket edges

With Rs of work facing, 3¼mm/No
10 needles and B, pick up and
K31 [31:35:35:39:39] sts along edge
of pocket.
1st row (Ws) K1, *P1, K1, rep from *
to end.
2nd row P1, *K1, P1, rep from * to
end.
Rep these 2 rows for 2cm/¾in. Cast
off in rib.

To make up

Press lightly under a dry cloth with
a warm iron. Join side and sleeve
seams. Sew cast-on edge of pocket
lining to top of ribbed welt. Sew
down ends of pocket edges. Fold
neckband in half to Ws and sl st in
place. Press seams.

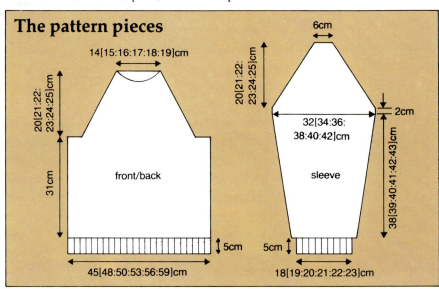

The pattern pieces

front/back
20[21:22:23:24:25]cm
31cm
14[15:16:17:18:19]cm
45[48:50:53:56:59]cm
5cm

sleeve
6cm
20[21:22:23:24:25]cm
32[34:36:38:40:42]cm
2cm
38[39:40:41:42:43]cm
5cm
18[19:20:21:22:23]cm

Zipped blouson-style jacket

This unusual zip-fronted jacket, suitable for either a man or woman, gives the effect of a woven fabric. Pockets, striped for fun, are placed vertically in the front sections and there are deep pleats on the shoulders.

All the ribbing is folded double to give a neat and comfortable fit and elastic is enclosed within the welt to help keep its shape.

Below: Experiment with colours in different combinations for totally different effects. Contrasting yarns give a striped look and soft toning ones give an all-over tweed effect.

8th row In B, P all the K sts and sl all the sl sts of previous row.

The 8 rows form patt and are rep throughout in a stripe sequence of 2 rows A, 4 rows D, 2 rows B, 2 rows A, 4 rows C, 2 rows B, 2 rows A, 4 rows E, 2 rows B, 2 rows A, 4 rows C and 2 rows B.

Back

With 4½mm/No 7 needles and A, beg at right side edge, cast on 51 [59:59:67] sts, working from side edge to side edge.

Working in patt as given, inc one st at armhole edge at beg of 3rd and every foll alt row 8 times in all. 59 [67:67:75] sts.

Cast on 42 sts (to the shoulder) at armhole edge at beg of foll alt row. 101 [109:109:117] sts.

Work a further 53 [61:69:77] rows in stripe patt, ending at neck edge.

Shape neck

K2 tog at beg of next and foll 4 alt rows. 96 [104:104:112] sts.

Cont in patt without shaping for 40 rows.

Inc one st at neck edge at beg of next and every foll alt row 5 times. 101 [109:109:117] sts.

Work 54 [62:70:78] rows in patt without shaping, ending at shoulder edge.

Shape armhole

Cast off 42 sts at beg of next row.

Dec one st at armhole edge on every foll alt row 8 times. Cast off.

Pocket linings

With 4½mm/No 7 needles and A, cast on 26 sts. Beg with a K row work 2 rows st st.

Working in a stripe sequence of 2 rows B, 2 rows A throughout, dec one st at beg and inc one st at end of every alt row 10 times.

Dec one st at beg *only* of every alt row until pocket measures 13cm/5in from beg.

Now reverse shaping by inc one st at beg of every alt row (the same edge as previous dec) until there are 26 sts.

Cont inc at beg of every alt row, at the same time dec one st at end of every alt row until pocket measures 26cm/10in from beg. Leave sts on holder.

Make 2nd pocket in same way reversing all the shaping.

Above: Detail of the shoulder pleat showing where to place it in relation to the armhole edge.

Sizes

To fit 89–91 [97–99:102–107:109–112]cm/35–36 [38–39:40–42:43–44]in bust/chest

Length to shoulder, 55.5 [59.5:59.5:63.5]cm/22 [23½:23½:25]in

Sleeve seam, 42.5 [45.5:45.5:47.5]cm/16¾ [18:18:18¾]in

The figures in [] refer to the 97–99/38–39, 102–107/40–42 and 109–112cm/43–44in sizes respectively

You will need

5 [5:6:6]×50g balls of Pingouin Confort (50% wool, 40% acrylic, 10% mohair) in main colour A

4 [4:5:5]×50g balls of Pingouin Type Shetland (100% wool) in contrast colour B

8 [8:9:9]×50g balls of Pingouin Tweede Rustique (63% wool, 22% acrylic, 15% mohair) in contrast colour C

3 [3:4:4] balls of Tweede Rustique in contrast colours D and E

One pair 3¼mm/No 10 needles

One pair 4½mm/No 7 needles

One 45 [50:50:55]cm/18 [20:20:22]in open-ended zip

Hip length 5cm/2in wide elastic

Tension

20 sts and 36 rows to 10cm/4in over patt worked on 4½mm/No 7 needles

Stitch pattern

1st row (Rs) In A, K to end.

2nd row In A, P to end.

3rd row Join in C, K1, *sl 1, K1, rep from * to end.

4th row In C, P all the K sts and sl all the sl sts of previous row.

5th row In C, P to end.

6th row In C, K to end. Break off C.

7th row Join in B, K2, *sl 1, K3, rep from * to last st, K1.

Right front

**With 4½mm/No 7 needles and B, beg at centre front edge, cast on 81 [89:89:97] sts.
K 2 rows in g st.
Change to A and work 2 rows st st. Beg with a 3rd row, work 14 rows in patt.**

Shape neck

Cont in patt, inc one st at beg of next and every alt row until there are 93 [101:101:109] sts, ending at neck edge.
Cast on 8 sts at beg of next row. 101 [109:109:117] sts.
Beg with a 2nd patt row, work 21 rows in patt, ending at neck edge.

Place pocket

Next row Patt across 55 [63:63:71] sts, cast off next 26 sts, work to end of row.
Next row Work to pocket opening, work across 26 sts of right pocket (the pocket which slopes downwards when held against work with st st inside), work to end of row.
Work a further 30 [38:46:54] rows in patt, ending at shoulder edge.

Shape armhole

Cast off 42 sts at beg of next row.
Dec one st at armhole edge on next and every foll alt row 8 times in all. 51 [59:59:67] sts. Cast off loosely.

Left front

Work as given for right front from ** to **.

Shape neck

Cont in patt, inc one st at end of next and every alt row until there are 93 [101:101:109] sts.
Cast on 8 sts at beg of next row. 101 [109:109:117] sts.
Beg with a 2nd patt row, work 23 rows in patt, ending at lower edge.

Place pocket

Next row Patt across 20 sts, cast off next 26 sts, work to end of row.
Now complete to match right front, reversing all shaping.

Sleeves

With 4½mm/No 7 needles and A cast on 12 sts, and work from side seam to side seam.
Working in pattern as given, work 4 rows.

Next row Cast on 12 sts, patt to end.
Next row Inc in first st, patt to end.
Working extra sts into patt, cast on at beg of next and every alt row 12 sts once, 5 sts 3 times and 24 [30:30:34] sts once, *at the same time* cont inc one st every alt row at armhole edge until there are 86 [92:92:96] sts, ending at armhole edge.
Keeping cuff edge straight, inc one st at armhole of every row until there are 105 [111:111:115] sts, then every alt row until there are 116 [122:122:126] sts.
Work 12 rows without shaping.
Keeping patt correct dec one st at armhole edge on next and every foll alt row until there are 105 [111:111:115] sts, then every row until 86 [92:92:96] sts rem, ending at cuff edge.
Dec one st at armhole edge on next and every foll alt row until there are 81 [87:87:91] sts, ending at cuff edge.
Cast off at the beg of next and every foll alt row 24 [30:30:34] sts once, 5 sts 3 times and 12 sts once, *at the same time* cont to dec at armhole edge every alt row until 24 sts rem, ending at sleeve seam edge.
Cast off 12 sts at beg of next row.
Work 3 rows without shaping.
Cast off.

Back welt

With Rs of work facing, 3¼mm/No 10 needles and A pick up and K108 [108:116:124] sts evenly along lower edge of back.
Working in stripes of one row A, one row B throughout work 10cm/4in K1, P1 rib, carrying yarns up side of work when changing colours, by using 2 separate balls of A and B.

Cast off loosely in rib.

Front welts

Work as given for back welt picking up 60 [60:68:76] sts along lower edge of each front.

Cuffs

Work as given for back welt picking up 58 sts along each sleeve edge.

Neckband

Join shoulder seams.
With Rs of work facing, 3¼mm/No 10 needles and A pick up 32 sts up right front neck (starting at the first row in A), 38 sts across back neck and 32 sts down left front neck (ending at last row in A). 102 sts.
Complete as given for back welt.

To make up

Do not press.
Sew in sleeves. Join side and sleeve seams.
Fold shoulder pleats on the 2nd stripe in Tweede Rustique from armhole edge as illustrated and stitch for about 19cm/7½in both at back and front.
Fold front edges to Ws along first stripe in Tweede Rustique. Pin in zip from just below rib at neck to halfway down welt. Backstitch into place.
Fold neckband and cuffs in half to Ws and slipstitch into place.
Sew each end of elastic to edges of zip at lower edge of jacket.
Fold welt in half to Ws over elastic and slipstitch into place.
Sew cast on edge of pocket to cast off sts of jacket front, placing Rs tog and backstitching to join.

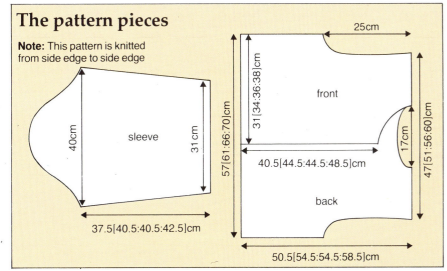

The pattern pieces

Note: This pattern is knitted from side edge to side edge

40cm

sleeve

31 cm

37.5[40.5:40.5:42.5]cm

25cm

31[34:36:38]cm

57[61:66:70]cm

front

40.5[44.5:44.5:48.5]cm

17cm

47[51:56:60]cm

back

50.5[54.5:54.5:58.5]cm

Man's three-colour jersey

The subtlest of toning colours are used to work the geometric shapes on the front of this jersey.
It has a comfortable dropped shoulder line and neat ribbed crew neckband.

Sizes

To fit 91 [97:102:107]cm/36 [38:40:42]in bust/chest
Length to shoulder, 64 [66:66:67]cm/25¼[26:26:26½]in
Sleeve seam, 49cm/19¼in
The figures in [] refer to the 97/38, 102/40 and 107cm/42in sizes respectively

You will need

14 [14:15:15]×40g balls of Poppleton Viva (75% acrylic, 15% mohair, 10% polyester) in main colour A
2 [2:2:2]×25g balls of Poppleton Rio (65% acrylic, 35% mohair) in each of contrast colours B and C
One pair 4mm/No 8 needles
One pair 5½mm/No 5 needles
Set of four 4mm/No 8 needles pointed at both ends

Tension

16 sts and 22 rows to 10cm/4in over st st worked on 5½mm/No 5 needles with A

Note

Use separate balls for each colour, always twisting yarns at back of work when changing colour to avoid a hole

Front

With 4mm/No 8 needles and A cast on 76 [80:84:88] sts.
1st row (Rs) K3, *P2, K2, rep from * to last st, K1.
2nd row K1, *P2, K2, rep from * to last 3 sts, P2, K1.
Rep these 2 rows for 10cm/4in, ending with a Rs row.
Next row (inc row) Rib 9 [10:10:11] sts, *pick up loop lying between sts and K tbl – **called M1**, rib 19 [20:21:22] sts, rep from * twice more, M1, rib 10 [10:11:11] sts. 80 [84:88:92] sts.**
Change to 5½mm/No 5 needles.

Left: This jersey would suit a woman too. Right: another colour scheme.

Beg with a K row and first row of chart, cont in st st reading Rs rows as K from right to left and Ws rows as P from left to right, until 104 rows have been completed.
Break off B and C. Cont with A only.

Shape neck

Next row K33 [34:36:37] sts, turn and leave rem sts on spare needle.
Complete left shoulder first.
Dec one st at neck edge on next 4 rows. 29 [30:32:33] sts.
Cont without shaping until work measures 7 [9:9:10]cm/2¾ [3½:3½:4]in from beg of neck shaping, ending at side edge.

Shape shoulder

Cast off at beg of next and every alt row 10 [10:11:11] sts twice and 9 [10:10:11] sts once.
With Rs of work facing, sl first 14 [16:16:18] sts on to a holder for centre front neck, rejoin A to rem sts and K to end.
Complete to match first side reversing all shaping.

Back

Work as given for front to **.
Change to 5½mm/No 5 needles.
Beg with a K row cont in st st with A only until back measures same as front to shoulders, ending with a P row.

Shape shoulders

Cast off at beg of next and every row 10 [10:11:11] sts 4 times and 9 [10:10:11] sts twice.
Leave rem 22 [24:24:26] sts on holder for centre back neck.

Chart for jersey front

size 1
size 2
size 3
size 4

colour A
colour B
colour C

size 1
size 2
size 3
size 4

Sleeves

With 4mm/No 8 needles and A cast
on 32 [36:36:40] sts.
Work 10cm/4in rib as given for
front, ending with a Rs row.
Next row (inc row) Rib 2 [4:1:3] sts,
*inc in next st, rib 3 [3:2:2] sts, rep
from * to last 2 [4:2:4] sts, inc in next
st, rib to end. 40 [44:48:52] sts.
Change to 5½mm/No 5 needles.
Beg with a K row cont in st st with A
only, inc one st at each end of 3rd
and every foll 6th row until there
are 66 [70:74:78] sts.
Cont without shaping until sleeve
measures 49cm/19¼in from beg, or
required length to underarm ending
with a P row.

Shape top

Cast off 4 sts at beg of next 8 rows.
Cast off rem 34 [38:42:46] sts.

Neckband

Join shoulder seams.
With Rs of work facing, set of four
4mm/No 8 needles and A, pick up
and K72 [80:80:88] sts evenly round
neck, including sts on holders.
Work 16 rounds in K2, P2 rib.
Cast off very loosely.

To make up

Press each piece lightly under a dry
cloth with a cool iron, omitting
ribbing.
With centre of sleeve top to
shoulder seams, set in sleeves.
Join side and sleeve seams. Press
seams.
Fold neckband in half to Ws and sl
st down.

The pattern pieces

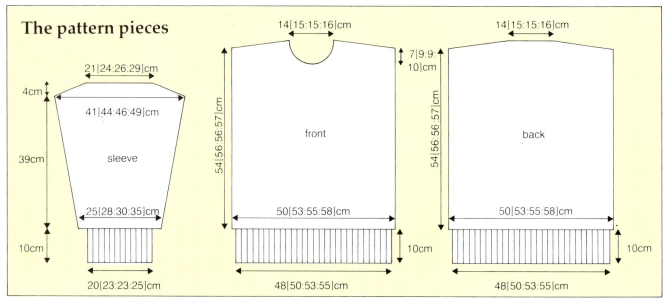

21[24:26:29]cm

4cm

41[44:46:49]cm

39cm   sleeve

25[28:30:35]cm

10cm

20[23:23:25]cm

14[15:15:16]cm

7[9:9:
10]cm

54[56:56:57]cm

front

50[53:55:58]cm

10cm

48[50:53:55]cm

14[15:15:16]cm

54[56:56:57]cm

back

50[53:55:58]cm

10cm

48[50:53:55]cm

Fisherman's rib jerseys for the family

Knit one of these cosy fisherman's rib classics for any member of your family. The pattern is given in a large range of sizes suitable for men, women and children.

The main pattern is formed by working every alternate stitch into the row below, which makes an attractive, raised rib.

A pattern for a matching scarf in the same stitch is also included.

Sizes

To fit 71 [76:81:87:91:97:102]cm/28 [30:32:34:36:38:40]in chest/bust
Length to centre back neck, 47 [51:55:58:61:63:65]cm/18½ [20:21¾: 22¾:24:24¾:25½]in
Sleeve seam, 37 [40:43:45:46:47: 48]cm/14½ [15¾:17:17¾:18:18½: 19]in
The figures in [] refer to the 76/30, 81/32, 87/34, 91/36, 97/38 and 102cm/ 40in sizes respectively

You will need

Jersey 9 [10:12:13:15:16:17]×50g
  balls of Emu Finlandia (100% wool)
Scarf 6 balls of same including fringe
One pair 4½mm/No 7 needles
One pair 5½mm/No 5 needles
Set of four 4½mm/No 7 needles pointed at both ends

Tension

13 sts and 28 rows to 10cm/4in over patt worked on 5½mm/No 5 needles, noting that fisherman's rib takes extra rows

Back

With 4½mm/No 7 needles cast on 53 [55:59:63:65:69:73] sts.
1st row (Rs) P1, *K1, P1, rep from * to end.
2nd row K1, *P1, K1, rep from * to end.
Rep these 2 rows for 5 [5:5:6:6:7: 7]cm/2 [2:2:2¼:2¼:2¾:2¾]in, ending with a 2nd row.
Change to 5½mm/No 5 needles.
Commence patt.
1st row (Rs) K1, *K into the loop below the next st on left-hand needle and allow st to drop off needle – **called K1B**, K1, rep from * to end.
2nd row K2, *K1B, K1, rep from * to last st, K1.
These 2 rows form patt and are rep throughout.
Cont in patt until work measures 30 [33:35:37:39:40:41]cm/11¾ [13:13¾: 14½:15¼:15¾:16¼]in from beg, ending with a Ws row.

Shape armholes

Cast off 2 [2:3:3:4:4:5] sts at beg of next 2 rows.
Dec one st at each end of next and every foll 4th row until 39 sts rem, ending with a Ws row.
Dec one st at each end of next and every foll alt row until 13 [15:17:19: 19:21:21] sts rem, ending with a Ws row.
Leave rem sts on holder for centre back neck.

Pocket lining

With 5½mm/No 5 needles cast on 36 [38:38:43:45:45:45] sts. Beg with a K row cont in st st until work measures 3 [4:4:4:5:5:5]cm/1¼ [1½: 1½:1½:2:2:2]in from beg. Leave sts on a holder.

Front

Work as given for back until front measures 8 [9:9:10:11:12:12]cm/3¼ [3½:3½:4:4¼:4¾:4¾]in from beg, ending with a Ws row.

Place pocket

Next row Patt 12 [12:14:14:14:16:18] sts, sl next 29 [31:31:35:37:37:37] sts on to a spare needle, K across sts of pocket lining, patt to end.
Next row Patt 12 [12:14:14:14:16:18] sts, P36 [38:38:43:45:45:45] sts, patt to end.
Cont in patt as now set, keeping pocket lining sts in st st, for a further 8 [9:10:11:12:12:13]cm/3¼ [3½:4:4¼:4¾:4¾:5]in, ending with a Ws row and dec 7 [7:7:8:8:8:8] sts evenly across pocket lining sts on last row. Do not break off yarn.
With Rs of work facing, return to sts on spare needle, rejoin yarn and cont in patt as set on these sts for 8 [9:10:11:12:12:13]cm/3¼ [3½:4:4¼: 4¾:4¾:5]in, ending with a Ws row. Break off yarn.

Join front and pocket lining

With Rs of work facing, return to where sts were left, patt 12 [12:14: 14:14:16:18] sts, place pocket front in front of pocket lining sts and work tog one st from each needle across pocket, then patt to end. 53 [55:59:63:65:69:73] sts.
Cont in patt as given for back until 27 [31:31:35:35:39:39] sts rem in armhole shaping, ending with a Ws row.

Shape neck

Next row K2 tog, patt 9 [10:10:11: 11:12:12] sts, turn and leave rem sts on spare needle.
Complete left side first.
Next row Patt to end.
Next row K2 tog, patt to last 2 sts K2 tog.
Rep last 2 rows twice more, then cont to dec at armhole edge only until 2 sts rem. K2 tog and fasten off.

The pattern pieces

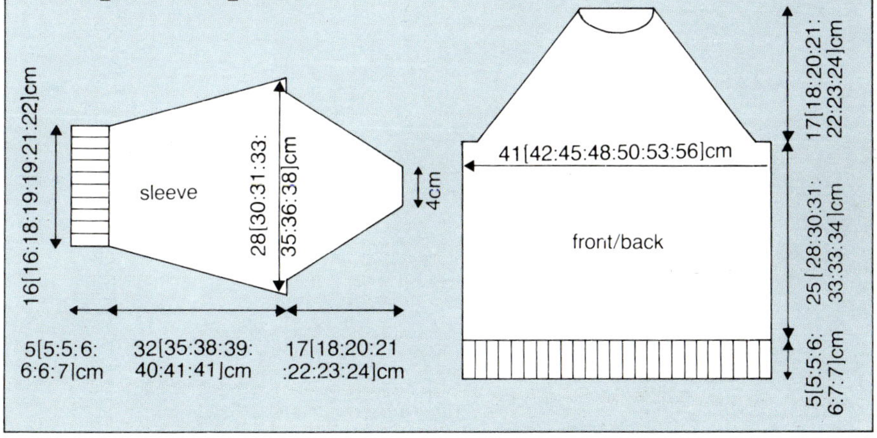

10[11:13:15:15:16:16]cm

17[18:20:21: 22:23:24]cm

41[42:45:48:50:53:56]cm

front/back

25[28:30:31: 33:33:34]cm

16[16:18:19:19:21:22]cm

sleeve

28[30:31:33: 35:36:38]cm

4cm

5[5:5:6: 6:6:7]cm   32[35:38:39: 40:41:41]cm   17[18:20:21 :22:23:24]cm

5[5:5:6: 6:7:7]cm

Above: Knit a scarf to match or contrast with the jersey, or make just the scarf on its own.

Left: Knitted from 100% wool these extra warm jerseys have raglan shaping at the armholes and a pouch pocket at centre front. The lining of the pocket is worked in plain stocking stitch to reduce bulk.

With Rs of work facing, sl first 5 [7:7:9:9:11:11] sts on holder for centre front neck, rejoin yarn to rem sts, patt to last 2 sts, K2 tog. Complete to match first side, reversing shapings.

Sleeves

With 4½mm/No 7 needles cast on 21 [21:23:25:25:27:29] sts. Work 5 [5:5:6:6:6:7]cm/2 [2:2:2¼:2¼:2¼:2¾]in rib as given for back, ending with a 2nd row.

Change to 5½mm/No 5 needles. Cont in patt as given for back, inc one st at each end of 5th and every foll 10th row until there are 37 [39:41:43:45:47:49] sts, working extra sts into patt.

Cont without shaping until work measures 37 [40:43:45:46:47:48]cm/ 14½ [15¾:17:17¾:18:18½:19]in from beg, ending with a Ws row.

Shape top

Cast off 2 [2:3:3:4:4:5] sts at beg of next 2 rows. Work 2 rows. Dec one st at each end of next and every foll 4th row until 15 [17:13:13: 9:11:7] sts rem, ending with a Ws row.

Dec one st at each end of next and every foll alt row until 5 sts rem, ending with a Ws row. Leave rem sts on a holder.

Neckband

Join raglan seams.

With Rs of work facing and set of four 4½mm/No 7 needles, patt across sts of back neck and left sleeve, K2 tog at seam, pick up and K12 [12:14:14:16:16:18] sts down left front neck, patt across front neck sts on holder, pick up and K12 [12:14: 14:16:16:18] sts up right front neck, patt across sts of right sleeve, K last st of sleeve tog with first st of back neck. 50 [54:60:64:68:72:76] sts. Cont in rounds of K1, P1 rib for 4 [5:5:5:6:6:6]cm/1½ [2:2:2:2¼:2¼: 2¼]in. Cast off very loosely in rib.

Pocket edges

With Rs of work facing and 4½mm/ No 7 needles, pick up and K21 [23:25:27:29:29:31] sts evenly along pocket edge.

Work 2 [2:2:3:3:3:3]cm/¾ [¾:¾:1¼: 1¼:1¼:1¼]in rib as given for back. Cast off in rib.

Scarf

With 5½mm/No 5 needles cast on 31 sts. Work in fisherman's rib patt as given for back until work measures 150cm/59¼in from beg. Cast off in patt.

To make up

Do not press.

Jersey Join side and sleeve seams. Fold neckband in half to Ws and sl st down. Sew down pocket lining and pocket edges.

Scarf Cut yarn into lengths of 30cm/11¾in. Taking 4 strands tog each time, work a knotted fringe along each end of scarf. Trim fringe.

Below: Detail of rib pattern on scarf.

Man's striped jersey

Sizes

To fit 97 [102:107]cm/38 [40:42]in chest
Length to back neck, 76 [77:78]cm/ 30 [30¼:30¾]in
Sleeve seam, 50cm/19¾in adjustable
The figures in [] refer to the 102/40 and 107cm/42in sizes respectively

You will need

13 [13:14]×50g balls of Patons Shetland Chunky in main colour M, (50% acrylic, 25% nylon, 25% wool)
About 25×13.7m/14¾yd skeins of Coats/Anchor Tapisserie wool in assorted colours C, (100% wool)
Or oddments of Patons Shetland Chunky in assorted colours to give a total of 150g, C
One pair 4½mm/No 7 needles
One pair 6mm/No 4 needles
Set of four 4½mm/No 7 needles

Tension

15 sts and 20 rows to 10cm/4in over st st worked with M on 6mm/No 4 needles

Note

Only the Tapisserie wool is used double throughout. Colours are used at random in any order but take care to match back and front body and raglan stripes

Back

With 4½mm/No 7 needles and M, cast on 83 [87:91] sts.
1st row (Rs) K1, *P1, K1, rep from * to end.
2nd row P1, *K1, P1, rep from * to end.
Rep these 2 rows for 4cm/1½in, ending with a 2nd row.
Change to 6mm/No 4 needles. Beg with a K row work 2 rows st st.
1st row K3 M, *1 C, 3 M, rep from * to end.
Beg with a P row work 3 rows st st with M.
5th Row K1 M, *1 C, 3 M, rep from * to last 2 sts, 1 C, 1 M.
Beg with a P row work 3 rows st st with M.
These 8 rows form striped patt,

using colours as required. Cont until work measures 53cm/20¾in from beg, ending with a P row.

Shape armholes

Cast off 5 sts at beg of next 2 rows.
Next row K2, sl 1, K1, psso, K to last 4 sts, K2 tog, K2.
Next row P to end.
Rep last 2 rows until 27 [29:31] sts rem, ending with a P row. Leave sts on holder for back neck.

Front

Beg with a 5th patt row work as given for back until 43 [45:47] sts rem in armhole shaping, ending with a P row.

Shape neck

Next row K2, sl 1, K1, psso, K11, turn and leave rem sts on holder. Complete left side first.
Next row P to end.
Next row K2, sl 1, K1, psso, K to last 2 sts, K2 tog.
Rep last 2 rows 4 times more, then P one row.
Next row K2, sl 1, K1, psso.
Next row P3.
Next row K1, sl 1, K1, psso.
Next row P2.
Cast off.
With Rs of work facing, leave first 13 [15:17] sts on holder for front neck, rejoin yarn to rem sts, K to last 4 sts, K2 tog, K2.
Next row P to end.
Next row Sl 1, K1, psso, K to last 4 sts, K2 tog, K2.
Complete to match left side, reversing shaping.

Sleeves

With 4½mm/No 7 needles and M,

cast on 31 [33:35] sts. Work 4cm/1½in rib as for back, ending with a 2nd row and inc 4 sts evenly in last row. 35 [37:39] sts.
Change to 6mm/No 4 needles. Beg with a K row work 2 rows st st.
1st row (Rs)K3 [2:3] M, *1 C, 3 M, rep from * to last 4 [3:4] sts, 1 C, 3 [2:3] M.
Cont in patt as now set, inc one st at each end of 5th patt row and every foll 6th row until there are 63 [65:67] sts. Cont without shaping until sleeve measures 50cm/19¾in from beg, or required length to underarm ending with same patt row as at back and front armholes.

Shape top

Keeping striped patt as back and front correct, cast off 5 sts at beg of next 2 rows. Dec one st at each end of next and every alt row as given for back until 7 sts rem, ending with a P row.
Leave sts on holder.

Neckband

Join raglan seams. With Rs facing, set of four 4½mm/No 7 needles and M, K across sts of back neck and left sleeve top K2 tog at seam, pick up and K8 sts down left front neck, K across front neck sts, pick up and K8 sts up right front neck, K across sts of right sleeve top K last st of sleeve tog with first st of back neck. 68 [72:76] sts.
Work 3cm/1¼in in rounds of K1, P1 rib. Cast off in rib.

To make up

Do not press. Join side and sleeve seams.

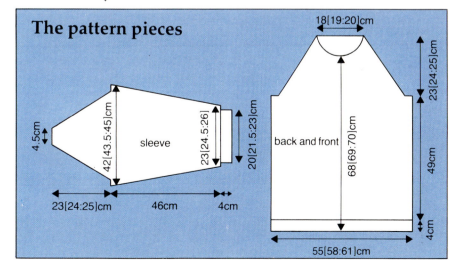

The pattern pieces

sleeve

back and front

4.5cm
42[43.5:45]cm
23[24.5:26]cm
20[21.5:23]cm
23[24:25]cm
46cm
4cm
18[19:20]cm
23[24:25]cm
68[69:70]cm
49cm
4cm
55[58:61]cm

Designer jersey for a man or woman

This easy-fitting simple shape can be adapted in a variety of ways. Try using any stitch patterns of your own choice for the body, except for lace patterns which will stretch out, or cable patterns that will pull in, thus distorting the shape.

Instead of using four colours as here, try it on one colour only; just add together the quantities for each colour to arrive at the total.

For more variety, instead of working the sleeve top and yoke in a cable pattern, use an Aran pattern.

As a further alternative use any firm, smooth-textured yarn of your choice, working out your own tension to arrive at the number of stitches and rows needed to achieve the given measurements.

Size

To fit 86-97cm/34-38in bust/chest
Length to shoulder, 68cm/26¾in
Sleeve seam, 45cm/17¾in

You will need

6×50g balls of Scheepjeswol Luzern (55% wool, 45% acrylic) in main colour A
5 balls each of same in contrast colours B and C
3 balls of same in contrast colour D
One pair 3¾mm/No 9 needles
One pair 4½mm/No 7 needles
One cable needle

Tension

20 sts and 26 rows to 10cm/4in over st st worked on 4½mm/No 7 needles

Note

Use separate balls of yarn for each colour and twist yarns together on Ws when changing colour

Diamond cable

Multiples of 11 sts.
1st row (Rs) *P3, sl next st on to cable needle and hold at back of work, K1 tbl then P1 from cable needle – **called cr2R**, K1, sl next st on to cable needle and hold at front of work, P1 then K1 tbl from cable needle – **called cr2L**, P3, rep from * to end.
2nd and every alt row P all K sts and K all P sts of previous row.
3rd row *P2, cr2R, K1, P1, K1, cr2L,

P2, rep from * to end.
5th row *P1, cr2R, (K1, P1) twice, K1, cr2L, P1, rep from * to end.
7th row *Cr2R, (K1, P1) 3 times, K1, cr2L, rep from * to end.
9th row *Cr2L, (P1, K1) 3 times, P1, cr2R, rep from * to end.
11th row *P1, cr2L, (P1, K1) twice, P1, cr2R, P1, rep from * to end.
13th row *P2, cr2L, P1, K1, P1, cr2R, P2, rep from * to end.
15th row *P3, cr2L, P1, cr2R, P3, rep from * to end.
16th row As 2nd.
These 16 rows form the pattern.

Single cable to the right

Multiples of 6 sts.
1st row (Rs) K.
2nd row P.
Rep 1st and 2nd rows twice more.
7th row Sl next 3 sts on to cable needle and hold at back of work, K3 then K3 from cable needle.
8th row As 2nd.
These 8 rows form the pattern.

Single cable to the left

Multiples of 6 sts.
1st row (Rs) K.
2nd row P.
Rep 1st and 2nd rows twice more.
7th row Sl next 3 sts on to cable needle and hold at front of work, K3 then K3 from cable needle.
8th row As 2nd.
These 8 rows form the pattern.

Seeded rib

Multiples of 4 sts plus 2.
1st row (Rs) K2, *P1, K3, rep from * to end.
2nd row K1, *P1, K3, rep from * to last st, P1.
These 2 rows form the pattern.

Basket pattern back/front

Multiples of 6 sts plus 4.
1st row (Rs) K.
2nd row P.
3rd row P1, *K2, P4, rep from * to last 3 sts, K2, P1.
4th row K1, *P2, K4, rep from * to last 3 sts, P2, K1.
5th and 6th rows As 3rd and 4th.
7th and 8th rows As 1st and 2nd.
9th row *P4, K2, rep from * to last 4 sts, P4.
10th row *K4, P2, rep from * to last 4 sts, K4.

11th and 12th rows As 9th and 10th.
These 12 rows form the pattern.

Basket pattern for sleeves

Multiples of 6 sts.
1st row (Rs) K.
2nd row P.
3rd row *K1, P4, K1, rep from * to end.
4th row *P1, K4, P1, rep from * to end.
5th and 6th rows As 3rd and 4th.
7th and 8th rows As 1st and 2nd.
9th row *P2, K2, P2, rep from * to end.
10th row *K2, P2, K2, rep from * to end.
11th and 12th rows As 9th and 10th.
These 12 rows form the pattern.

Diagonal pattern

Multiples of 4 sts plus 2.
1st row (Rs) K2, *P2, K2, rep from * to end.
2nd row P2, *K2, P2, rep from * to end.
3rd row P1, *K2, P2, rep from * to last st, K1.
4th row As 3rd.
5th row As 2nd.
6th row As 1st.
7th row K1, *P2, K2, rep from * to last st, P1.
8th row K1, *P2, K2, rep from * to last st, P1. These 8 rows form patt.

Back

With 3¾mm/No 9 needles and A cast on 101 sts.
1st row (Rs) K1, *P1, K1, rep from * to end.
2nd row P1, *K1, P1, rep from * to end.
Rep these 2 rows for 5cm/2in, ending with a 2nd row and inc one st at end of last row. 102 sts.
Change to 4½mm/No 7 needles. Commence patt.
1st row (Rs) With B, patt 34 sts as 1st row of seeded rib, with C, patt 34 sts as 1st row of basket patt, with D, patt 34 sts as 1st row of diagonal patt.
2nd row With D, patt 34 sts as 2nd row of diagonal patt, with C, patt 34 sts as 2nd row of basket patt, with B, patt 34 sts as 2nd row of seeded rib.
3rd row With B, patt 34 sts as 3rd row of seeded rib, with C, patt 34

The textural contrast between the stitch
patterns used on this jersey are
particularly striking if the garment is
knitted in a single colour such as a
creamy Aran-style yarn.

sts as 3rd row of basket patt, with D, patt 34 sts as 3rd row of diagonal patt.
Cont in patt as now set until work measures 43cm/17in from beg, ending with a Ws row.

Shape armholes

Keeping patt correct throughout, cast off 12 sts at beg of next 2 rows. 78 sts.
Cont in patt without shaping until armholes measure 15cm/6in from beg, ending with a Ws row.
Cast off loosely.

Front

Work as given for back.

Sleeves and yoke

With spare 4½mm/No 7 needle cast on 30 sts with C and 30 sts with B. Leave for time being.
With 3¾mm/No 9 needles and A cast on 49 sts. Work 5cm/2in rib as given for back, ending with a 1st row.
Next row (inc) (Rib 1, pick up loop lying between needles and K tbl – **called M1**) 3 times, (inc in next st, M1) 5 times, (rib 1, M1) 13 times, (inc in next st, M1) 7 times, (rib 1, M1) 13 times, (inc in next st, M1) 5 times, (rib 1, M1) twice, rib 1. 114 sts.
Change to 4½mm/No 7 needles. Commence patt.
1st row (Rs) With B, patt 30 sts as 1st row of basket patt, with A, P6, patt 11 sts as 1st row of diamond cable, P7, patt 6 sts as 1st row of single cable to the right, P7, patt 11 sts as 1st row of diamond cable, P6, with C, patt 30 sts as 1st row of diagonal rib.
2nd row With C, patt 30 sts as 2nd row of diagonal rib, with A, K6, patt 11 sts as 2nd row of diamond cable, K7, patt 6 sts as 2nd row of single cable, K7, patt 11 sts as 2nd row of diamond cable, K6, with B, patt 30 sts as 2nd row of basket patt.
Cont in patt as now set until sleeve measures 46cm/18in from beg, ending with 6th row of diamond cable patt.

Shape armholes

Keeping patt correct, cast off 30 sts at beg of next 2 rows. 54 sts. Work a further 18 rows patt, ending with 10th row of diamond cable.

Divide for neck

Next row (Rs) Patt 20 sts, turn and leave rem sts on spare needle.
Cont in patt without shaping for a further 23cm/9in, ending with a 4th row of diamond cable. Leave sts on spare needle.
With Rs of work facing, rejoin yarn to rem sts, cast off centre 14 sts, patt to end.
Complete to match first side.
Next row With Rs of work facing cast on 14 sts for centre, break off yarn, take up first set of sts, patt across these sts, patt across sts just cast on as foll, P4, K6, P4, patt to end. 54 sts.
Work 19 rows patt without shaping, ending with 10th row.
Next row Take up sts cast on with C, work across these sts as 3rd row of diagonal patt, patt 54 sts in A, take up sts cast on in B, patt across these sts as 9th row basket patt. 114 sts.
Cont in patt as now set without shaping until coloured sections measure 46cm/18in, ending with 16th row of diamond cable.
Change to 3¾mm/No 9 needles. Cont with A only.
Next row (dec) (K2 tog) 3 times, (K3 tog) 5 times, (K2 tog) 13 times, (K3 tog) 7 times, (K2 tog) 13 times, (K3 tog) 5 times, (K2 tog) twice, K1. 49 sts.
Beg with a 2nd row work 5cm/2in rib as given for back, ending with a 2nd row. Cast off evenly in rib.

Neck border

With Rs of work facing and 3¾mm/No 9 needles and A pick up and K55 sts across straight edge of neck.
1st row P2, *K1, P1, rep from * to last st, P1.
2nd row K2, *P1, K1, rep from * to last st, K1.
Rep last 2 rows for 3.5cm/1½in, ending with a 1st row. Cast off loosely in rib.
Rep for other side of neck.

To make up

Do not press.
Overlap neck borders and sew in position taking in fullness over cables.
Join yoke to back and front. Join side and sleeve seams.

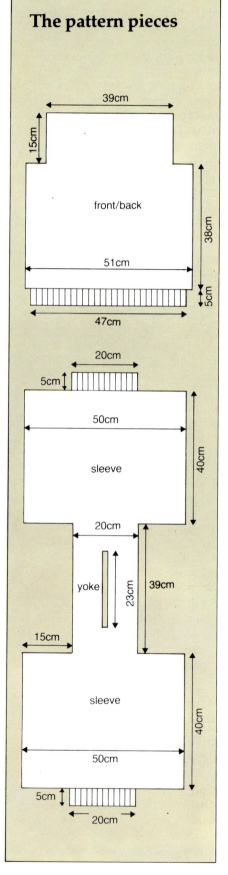

The pattern pieces

39cm
15cm
front/back
38cm
51cm
5cm
47cm

20cm
5cm
50cm
40cm
sleeve
20cm
yoke
23cm
39cm
15cm
sleeve
40cm
50cm
5cm
20cm

Choosing the right yarn

Every effort has been made to ensure that the colours and qualities shown in the knitting patterns are available at the time of publication. However, the spinners (yarn manufacturers) introduce new ranges every year and reserve the right to withdraw colours in each range, or a complete range, at any time entirely at their discretion. They assess each range at regular intervals and change the yarns according to fashions and sales. When possible, it is wise to use the yarn recommended for each design featured in this book but do remember that many of the yarns are unique and will not be interchangeable without adjusting the pattern.

If you have difficulty in obtaining the correct yarn, contact the spinner at the address shown below or use the mail order address if there is one given. The yarns used in this book are given alphabetically under each spinner together with manufacturer's recommended tension and aftercare advice. If the recommended yarn is unobtainable, make a note of the number of stitches and rows to a 10cm/4in square and look for another yarn with the same tension. If a yarn is near to this size, you could use a coarser or finer needle to achieve the required tension, check by knitting a tension square. Remember also, that if you substitute one yarn for another, the texture may not be the same as the original and the quantities and aftercare may vary.

Argyll

UK: Argyll Wools Ltd, PO Box 15, Priestly Mills, Pudsey, West Yorkshire LS28 9LT

Cotton On (p 20)
Recommended tension 22 sts and 30 rows to 10cm/4in over st st worked on 3¾mm/No 9 needles.
Aftercare Hand wash only (30°C), cool iron.

Ferndale Double Knitting (p 57)
Recommended tension 22 sts and 30 rows to 10cm/4in over st st worked on 4mm/No 8 needles.
Aftercare Hand or machine wash (6), do not iron.

D.M.C.

UK: Dunlicraft Ltd, Pullman Road, Wigston, Leicestershire LE8 2DY.
Mail order: The Needlewoman, 15 Station Road, London E4.
Australia: Olivier (Australia) PTY Ltd, 47-57 Collins Street, Alexandria, New South Wales 2015.
S. Africa: S. African Threads & Cottons Ltd., 56 Barrack Street, Cape Town 8001.

Pearl Cotton No 4 (p 11)
Recommended tension 26 sts and 34 rows to 10cm/4in over st st worked on 3¼mm/No 10 needles.
Aftercare Warm hand wash, cold rinse, dry flat, dry clean Ⓐ, warm iron under a damp cloth.

Emu Wools

UK: Leeds Road, Greengate, Bradford, West Yorkshire.
Australia: The Needlewoman, Karingal, Grove, Tasmania 7106.
S. Africa: Patons & Baldwins S. Africa PTY Ltd, PO Box 33, Randfontein 1760, Transvaal.

Finlandia (p 109)
Recommended tension 16 sts and 22 rows to 10cm/4in over st st worked on 5½mm/No 5 needles.
Aftercare Hand wash only (40°C), dry clean Ⓟ, warm iron.

Guernsey (p 75)
Recommended tension 28 sts and 36 rows to 10cm/4in over st st worked on 3mm/No 11 needles.
Aftercare Hand wash only (40°C), dry flat, do not wring, dry clean Ⓟ, warm iron.

Hayfield

UK: Hayfield Textiles Ltd, Hayfield Mills, Glusburn, Keighley, West Yorkshire BD20 8QP.
Australia: Panda Yarns (International) PTY Ltd, 17-27 Brunswick Road, E. Brunswick, Victoria 3057.
S. Africa: A & H Agencies, 392 Commissioner Street, Fairview, Johannesburg 2094.

Brig Aran (p 81)
Recommended tension 18 sts and 24 rows to 10cm/4in over st st worked on 4½mm/No 7 needles.
Aftercare Hand wash only (40°C), warm iron.

Thermoknit for Aran (p 49)
Recommended tension 18 sts and 22 rows to 10cm/4in over st st worked on 5mm/No 6 needles.
Aftercare Hand wash (40°C) or machine wash (6), do not dry clean, bleach or iron.

Neveda

UK: Neveda Hand Knitting Yarns, Smallwares Ltd., 17 Galena Road, King Street, Hammersmith, London W6 0LU.

Brenda (p9, 24)
Recommended tension 18 sts and 24 rows to 10cm/4in over st st worked on 4mm/No 8 needles
Aftercare Hand or machine wash (30°C), dry clean Ⓟ, cool iron.

Jaeger

UK: Jaeger Hand Knitting Ltd, Alloa, FK10 1EG, Clackmannanshire, Scotland.
Mail order: Woolfayre, 120 High Street, Northallerton, Yorkshire.
Australia: Coats Patons (Australia) Ltd, 321-355 Ferntree Gulley Road, PO Box 110, Mount Waverley, Victoria 3149.
S. Africa: Patons & Baldwins S. Africa PTY Ltd, PO Box 33, Randfontein, 1760, Transvaal.

Wool/Silk (p 30)
Recommended tension 28 sts and 36 rows to 10cm/4in over st st worked on 3¼mm/No 10 needles.

Lister-Lee

UK: George Lee & Sons Ltd, Whiteoak Mills, PO Box 37, Wakefield WF2 9SF, Yorkshire.
Australia: M J Shaw, Butterfield Holding PTY Ltd, PO Box 518, Manuka, ACT 2603.

Shetland Chunky (p 113)
Recommended tension 15 sts and 20 rows to 10cm/4in over st st worked on 6mm/No 4 needles.
Aftercare Hand wash (40°C), machine wash (7), dry clean Ⓐ, do not bleach or iron.

Patons & Baldwins Ltd

UK: Alloa FK10 1EG, Clackmannanshire, Scotland.
Mail order: Woolfayre, 120 High Street, Northallerton, Yorkshire.

Australia: Coats Patons (Australia) Ltd, 321-355 Ferntree Gulley Road, PO Box 110, Mount Waverley, Victoria 3149.
S. Africa: Patons & Baldwins S. Africa PTY Ltd, PO Box 33, Randfontein 1760, Transvaal.

Clansman 4 ply (p 67)
Recommended tension 28 sts and 36 rows to 10cm/4in over st st worked on 3¼mm/No 10 needles. **Aftercare** Hand wash (40°C), machine wash (5), dry clean (A), warm iron, do not bleach.

Grampian Double Knitting (p 101)
Recommended tension 24 sts and 32 rows to 10cm/4in over st st worked on 3¾mm/No 9 needles. **Aftercare** Hand or machine wash (40°C), cool iron.

Phildar (UK) Ltd
UK: 4 Gambrel Road, Westgate Industrial Estate, Northamptonshire.
Mail order: Ries Wools, 243 High Holborn, London WC1.

Dedicace (p 39)
Recommended tension 21 sts and 30 rows to 10cm/4in over st st worked on 3¾mm/No 9 needles. **Aftercare** Hand or machine wash (30°C), dry clean (A), cool iron.

Kadischa (p 60)
Recommended tension 13 sts and 19 rows to 10cm/4in over st st worked on 6mm/No 4 needles. **Aftercare** Hand or machine wash (30°C), dry clean (A), warm iron, do not bleach.

Luxe (p 15)
Recommended tension 30 sts and 40 rows to 10cm/4in over st st worked on 2¼mm/No 13 needles. **Aftercare** Hand or machine wash (40°C), dry clean (A), do not bleach.

Pingouin
UK: French Wools (Pingouin) Ltd, 7-11 Lexington Street, London W1.

Biais de Coton (p 17)
Recommended tension 10 sts and 14 rows to 10cm/4in over st st worked on 10mm/No 000 needles. **Aftercare** Hand wash only (30°C), dry clean (A), hot iron.

Confort (p 103)
Recommended tension 23 sts and 28 rows to 10cm/4in over st st worked on 3¾mm/No 9 needles. **Aftercare** Hand or machine wash (40°C), dry clean (A), warm iron, do not bleach.

Pingouin Corrida 3 (p 96)
Recommended tension 28 sts and 37 rows to 10cm/4in over st st worked on 3mm/No 11 needles. **Aftercare** Hand or machine wash (30°C), dry clean (A), cool iron.

Mohair (p 36, 55)
Recommended tension 17sts and 22 rows to 10cm/4in over st st worked on 4½mm/No 7 needles. **Aftercare** Hand wash only, dry clean (A), warm iron.

Oued (p 35)
Recommended tension 24 sts and 36 rows to 10cm/4in over st st worked on 3¾mm/No 9 needles.

Tweede Rustique (p 103)
Recommended tension 13 sts and 16 rows to 10cm/4in over st st worked on 6mm/No 4 needles. **Aftercare** Hand wash only (30°C), dry clean (A), cool iron.

Type Shetland (p103)
Recommended tension 23 sts and 28 rows to 10cm/4in over st st worked on 4mm/No 8 needles. **Aftercare** Hand or machine wash (30°C), dry clean (A), warm iron.

Poppleton
UK: Richard Poppleton and Sons Ltd, Albert Mills, Horbury, Wakefield, West Yorkshire WF4 5NJ.

Guernsey 5 ply (p 79)
Recommended tension 28 sts and 36 rows to 10cm/4in over st st worked on 3mm/No 11 needles. **Aftercare** Hand wash only, warm iron.

Viva (p 107)
Rio (p 107)
Recommended tension 16 sts and 21 rows to 10cm/4in over st st worked on 5½mm/No 5 needles. **Aftercare** Hand wash only (30°C), cool iron.

Robin Wools Ltd
UK: Robin Mills, Idle, Bradford, West Yorkshire.
Australia: Mrs. Rosemary Mallet, The Needlewoman, Karingal, Grove, Huon, Tasmania.
S. Africa: E Brasch and Son, 57 La Rochelle Road, Trojan, Johannesburg.

Reward Double Double (p 98)
Reward Double Knitting (p 98)
Landscape Chunky (p 98)
Softspun (p 98)
Reward 4 ply (p98)
Recommended tension 16 sts and 22 rows to 10cm/4in over st st worked on 5½mm/No 5 needles for the Reward Double Double and Landscape Chunky.
16 sts and 20 rows to 10cm/4in over st st worked on 5½mm/No 5 needles for Softspun.
22 sts and 30 rows to 10cm/4in over st st worked on 4mm/No 8 needles for Reward Double Knitting.
28 sts and 36 rows to 10cm/4in over st st worked on 3¼mm/No 10 needles for Reward 4 ply.
Aftercare Hand or machine wash (40°C), dry clean (P), cool iron for Reward Double Double, Double Knitting and 4 ply and Landscape Chunky.
Handwash only the Softspun, dry clean (P), do not iron.

Scheepjeswol
UK: Aero Needles Group plc (Scheepjeswol), Box 2, Edward Street, Redditch, Worcs.
Australia: Thorobred Scheepjeswol MPTY Ltd, 726 High Street, East Kew, Melbourne 3102, Victoria.
S. Africa: Woolcraft Agencies MPTY Ltd, PO Box 17657, 2038 Hillbrow, Johannesburg.

Luzern (p 91, 114)
Recommended tension 20 sts and 26 rows to 10cm/4in over st st worked on 4½mm/No 7 needles. **Aftercare** Hand or machine wash (30°C), dry clean (A), do not iron.

Voluma (p 87)
Recommended tension 22 sts and 29 rows to 10cm/4in over st st worked on 4mm/No 8 needles. **Aftercare** Hand or machine wash (30°C), dry clean (A), do not iron.

Scotnord Ltd

UK: Broich Terrace, Crieff, Perthshire, Scotland PH7 3BW.

Alafoss Lopi Lyng (p 69)
Recommended tension 14 sts and 19 rows to 10cm/4in over st st worked on 6½mm/No 3 needles.
Aftercare Hand wash, warm iron.

Sirdar Ltd

UK: Flanshaw Lane, Alverthorpe, Wakefield, Yorkshire WF2 9ND.
Mail order: The Best Woolshop, 26-28 Frenchgate, Doncaster, South Yorkshire.
Australia: David L Rowl, Sirdar (Australia) PTY Ltd, PO Box 110, Mount Waverley, Victoria 3149.
S. Africa: Patons & Baldwins S. Africa PTY Ltd, PO Box 33, Randfontein 1760, Transvaal.

Country Style Double Knitting (p 29)
Recommended tension 24 sts and 30 rows to 10cm/4in over st st worked on 3¾mm/No 9 needles.
Aftercare Hand wash (40°C), dry clean, medium iron.

Wash 'n' Wear Double Crêpe (p 59, 95)
Recommended tension 24 sts and 30 rows to 10cm/4in over st st worked on 4mm/No 8 needles.
Aftercare Hand or machine wash (40°C), dry clean Ⓐ, warm iron under a dry cloth.

3 Suisses

UK: Filature de l'Espierres, Marlborough House, 38 Welford Road, Leicester LE2 7AA.

Suizasport (p 52)
Recommended tension 15 sts and 22 rows to 10cm/4in over st st worked on 4½mm/No 7 needles.
Aftercare Hand wash (40°C), machine wash (7), dry clean Ⓟ, do not iron.

Suizetta 4 ply (p 63)
Recommended tension 26 sts and 40 rows to 10cm/4in over st st worked on 3¾mm/No 12 needles.
Aftercare Hand wash (40°C), machine wash (7), dry clean Ⓟ, do not iron or bleach.

Sunbeam

UK: Richard Ingham & Co Ltd, Crawshaw Mills, Pudsey, Yorkshire.
Mail order: Woolfayre, 120 High Street, Northallerton, Yorkshire.

Aran Knit and Aran Tweed (p 45, 85)
Recommended tension 20 sts and 28 rows to 10cm/4in over st st worked on 4½mm/No 7 needles.
Aftercare Hand wash (30°C).

Trophy Double Knitting (p 71)
Recommended tension 24 sts and 30 rows to 10cm/4in over st st

worked on 4mm/No 8 needles.
Aftercare Hand wash, warm iron.

Wendy

UK: Carter and Parker Ltd, Gordon Mills, Guisley, West Yorkshire.
Australia: Craft Warehouse, 30 Guess Avenue, Arncliff, New South Wales, 2205.
S. Africa: Woolcraft Agencies, PO Box 17657, 2038 Hillbrow, Johannesburg.

Donna (p 33)
Recommended tension 18 sts and 26 rows to 10cm/4in over st st worked on 4½mm/No 7 needles.

Dolce (p 33)
Recommended tension 24 sts and 32 rows to 10cm/4in over st st worked on 4mm/No 8 needles.
Aftercare Hand wash only (30°C), cool dry press both yarns.

Fashion Crêpe Double Knitting
Choice Double Knitting (p 27)
Recommended tension 24 sts and 32 rows to 10cm/4in over st st worked on 4mm/No 8 needles.
Aftercare Hand wash (40°C), machine wash (6), cool dry press.

Mohair (p 43)
Recommended tension 16 sts and 24 rows to 10cm/4in over st st worked on 5mm/No 6 needles.
Aftercare Hand wash only, dry clean Ⓟ, warm iron.

Standard aftercare symbols

A tub indicates that the yarn can be hand or machine washed.

A hand in the tub means hand wash only.

A figure in the water shows the correct water temperature.
Numbers 1 to 9 above the water line denote washing machine programmes.

Where the tub is crossed through, dry-clean only.

An iron means the yarn can be pressed – one dot means cool; two dots medium and three dots hot.

Where the iron is crossed through do not attempt to press the yarn or you may ruin the fabric.

An empty circle means the yarn can be dry-cleaned.

An A inside the circle means dry-cleaning in all solvents.

The letter P means dry-cleaning only in certain solvents.

The letter F means dry-cleaning only in certain solvents.

Where the circle is crossed through do *not* dry-clean.

A triangle means that the yarn can be bleached.

Where the triangle is crossed through do not bleach.

Square signs denote drying instructions.

Three vertical lines in a square means drip dry.

One horizontal line in a square means dry flat.

A circle in a square means tumble dry.

A loop at the top of a square means dry on a line.

Index

Aran jerseys 81, 85
    moss stitch 83
Argyle waistcoat 96

Basket pattern 114
Batwing cardigan 9
    jersey 24, 54
Bobble and rib pattern 83
Bobbles 86
Butterfly pattern 17

Cable 114
    diamond 114
    lobster claw 86
    panel 49
Cable jacket 49
Cardigan:
    Fair Isle 63
    mohair, pierrot collar 36
    Norwegian-style 87
    striped batwing 9
    striped bobble 15
    tweed with woven clusters 45
    wavy striped, short sleeved 33

Designer jersey 114
Diamond cable 114
Dolly bobbin braid trim 98

Embroidered striped jersey 57
Entrelac jersey 35

Fair Isle cardigan 63
    slipover 65
Fife heart pattern 77
Fisherman's rib jersey 109
    scarf 111

Garter stitch and rib check jersey 26
Geometric design 91, 92
Guernsey 75, 79

Icelandic jersey 69

Jacket:
    cable 49
    zipped blouson-style 103
Jacquard yoked jersey 71
Jersey:
    Aran 81, 85
    batwing 24, 54
    cotton 11
    designer 114
    embroidered striped 57
    entrelac 43
    fisherman's rib 109
    flower motif 39
    garter stitch and rib checks 26
    geometric patterned 98
    guernsey 75, 79
    Icelandic 69
    jacquard-yoked 71
    Norwegian-style 91
    raglan-sleeved with pouch
    pocket 101
    random patterned 20
    random striped 113
    stitch sampler 52
    striped 59
    three-colour 107
    wavy striped, short sleeved 33
Lace patterned pullover 29
Ladder panel 79
Lobster claw cable 86

Mohair cardigan with pierrot
    collar 36
Mohair batwing jersey 54
Moss stitch diamond pattern 86

Norwegian-style cardigan 87
    jersey 91
    motifs 92-3

Peasant figure motif 92
Pine tree motif 87, 93
Positioning motifs on a garment 93
Pouch pocket jersey 101

Rag knit top 17
Raglan-sleeved jersey 101
Random patterned jersey 20
Random striped jersey 13

Scandinavian knitting 87-93
Scarf in fisherman's rib 111
Seeded rib 114
Seeding pattern 93
Sequinned party top 35
Sheringham herringbone and
    diamond pattern 77
Snowflake motif 87, 92
Stag motif 87, 92
Stitch sampler jersey 52
Striped batwing cardigan 9
    bobble cardigan 15
    reverse stocking stitch jersey 59

Three-colour jersey 107
Top:
    cricket-style cable pullover 95
    Fair Isle 65
    lace patterned 29
    picot edged sun 15
    rag knit 17
    sequinned party 35
Tree of Life pattern 83, 86

Waistcoat, Argyle 96
    double breasted 30
Wavy striped cardigan 33

Zigzag and bobble pattern 83
Zigzag panel 79
Zipped blouson-style jacket 103